TBI OR CTE

What the Hell is Wrong with Me?

Mark Tullius

VINCERE PRESS

Published by Vincere Press
65 Pine Ave., Ste. 806
Long Beach, CA 90802

TBI or CTE: What the Hell is Wrong with Me?
Copyright © 2021 by Mark Tullius

All rights reserved.
For information about permission to reproduce selections from this book, write to Permissions,
Vincere Press, 65 Pine Avenue Ste. 806,
Long Beach, CA 90802

Printed in the United States of America
First Edition
ISBN: 978-1-938475-86-3
Library of Congress Control Number: 2021912760

Photo and cover design by Karl Dominey
www.domineyphotography.com
Graphic Design by Florencio Ares aresjun@gmail.com

To Michael and Sara,
This book would not have been written if it were not for you opening your home and hearts to me. I will always appreciate this.

TBI OR CTE

What the Hell is Wrong with Me?

Table of Contents

Prologue 1
Chapter One 4
Chapter Two 10
Chapter Three 16
Chapter Four 20
Chapter Five 28
Chapter Six 39
Chapter Seven 51
Chapter Eight 62
Chapter Nine 72
Chapter Ten 83
Chapter Eleven 95
Chapter Twelve 108
Chapter Thirteen 123
TESTING AND SCANS
REVIEW
ABOUT THE AUTHOR
Out Now – TNTD: In the Wizard's Tower
Coming Soon from Vincere Press
Out Now from Vincere Press
Your Free Book is Waiting

Author's Note

I am not a scientist, doctor, health expert, or role model. I'm just a guy trying to find his best way through life. My goal is not to make you an expert on traumatic brain injuries or brain health. I'd much rather help you take an honest look at yourself and fill you with hope that you can improve your mental well-being.

Instead of a book filled with footnotes, you will find at the back of this book a list of all the books and websites I trusted for information. I encourage you to turn to those books for deeper explanations and to do your own research through other sources. We are all unique individuals and what works for me doesn't mean it will do the same for you. I wish you the best and hope this book helps you achieve improved quality of life.

Prologue

I should never own a gun again. That's what I just wrote down before I rationalized it away.

Not trusting myself with a gun is a scary thought, not the kind I should be having on a Saturday night after sitting front row for the Subversive Brazilian Jiu Jitsu tournament that my 10th Planet teammates dominated. I'd been tempted to use cannabis before the show, but I stayed sober intentionally, aware I was in a bad funk that needed to be examined instead of buried in smoke.

My anxiety is generally high around crowds, and loud music only amplifies it. My wife, Jen, was understanding and helped me deal at the venue: and while I did enjoy the matches, the downtime between them was where I realized there was a problem. Everyone else was talking and having a good time, and I was sitting there on the verge of tears, unable to explain what the hell I was experiencing.

Now, safe at home, waiting for my vaporizer to warm up, I understand part of the problem is depression. I have not been able to train much the past two years due to neck, back, and shoulder issues. Jiu jitsu has been a big part of my life and it sucks not being able to roll. Yet it goes even deeper than that.

News reports replay over and over in my mind. Junior Seau and Andre Waters killing themselves. Aaron Hernandez and his ravaged brain, convicted of the murder of a friend. I worry about Gary Goodridge and my numerous MMA and boxing friends dealing with varying degrees of brain damage. I consider my Brown University teammates who are in brain studies, one of whom I just spent three days with talking about what chronic traumatic encephalopathy (CTE) has done to his life and that he now only has a short time to live thanks to the combination of the neurodegenerative disease and acute myeloid leukemia. This man, who'd been told he had the frontal lobe of a 75-year-old, rattled off stories about myself that I can't recollect, my time at Brown, and much of my life, a messy blur.

I tell myself to get over it; I'm making this into something bigger than it needs to be. I haven't had nearly the amount of head trauma NFL players have had. Except for excessive caffeine and cannabis use, I've led a healthy lifestyle over the last decade. If my brain is deteriorating, surely I'd be aware of it.

But I can't deny that feeling's back. The one I've kept at bay through yoga, jiu jitsu, cognitive therapy, meditation, cold therapy, alcohol, and psychedelics. That dark, scary feeling I've had since I was ten, if not younger.

The mixture of rage and depression doesn't compute. It used to for the explosive child, the troubled teenager, the failed fighter, the loser who never did a damn thing with his degree. But I now have a beautiful life with a wonderful wife and two incredible children. We're set financially and everyone's healthy. I have close friends and a good support system. I'm publishing books at a nice pace and have found a balance between family and writing.

My vaporizer's warmed up so I turn it on, fill the bag with THC, breath it in. Load up another one because, holy shit, I want this feeling to go away.

But I stick with it, not willing to be a coward. Perhaps I lucked out and am blessed with a resilient brain, all those concussions and knockouts not having any lasting effect. Anyone that's read my fiction knows I'm a doom-and-gloom kind of guy, so maybe I'm just hardwired to focus on the negative. And even if all those brain injuries did cause problems, surely I'd gotten past them by now, especially with the treatment protocol I'm on.

But still, I must consider the symptoms.

Impulsive behavior: Guilty. Whether gambling, video games, or drugs, I can be an addict.

Memory loss: This one's not even funny. I can't tell you the number of times friends have shown me photos of events to prove that I was there. I blame it on the weed.

Difficulty planning and carrying out tasks: It takes me days to respond to emails. The littlest things are written down in hopes I'll one day do them.

Substance abuse: Thirty-one years of cannabis and counting, along with plenty of experimentation.

Emotional instability: It's not all the time. Usually I'm a fairly happy, even sweet guy, but it doesn't take a whole lot to rock the ship. One crappy night of sleep and my emotions are all over the place. I don't respond well to confrontation.

Depression or apathy: I never would've considered myself depressed until a year ago, but that's just due to the stigma behind the word. There's no denying that's what I'm experiencing.

Suicidal thoughts or behavior: I struggled with this most of my life, spending too many of my college nights with a gun in my mouth. It's not something I would ever do now that I have kids, and the urge has been dormant for the past decade, but even a trace of that self-destructiveness is something I must be aware of.

So regardless of the source of damage, there's something wrong with me. Whether it's from a traumatic brain injury (TBI), CTE, substance abuse, childhood scars, or good ole genetics, my brain is not in a great place.

But it's all good.

I'm going to fix it.

I have to.

Chapter One

I never wanted to write this book. In fact, during the writing of *Unlocking the Cage*, my exploration of mixed martial artists, I swore I'd never write nonfiction again. That process of traveling to 100 gyms and interviewing 400 fighters and coaches was one of the best things I've ever done, but it was also time-consuming, expensive, and physically taxing. And it took me away from my fiction, where I control whether the ending is happy or sad.

Prior to writing *UTC*, brain damage was the furthest thing from my mind. Back when I was fighting and playing football, I worried about weeklong headaches and speech problems, but I seemed to bounce back from all of them. The last blow to my head had been in 2004 and I felt fine, my high scores on the brain-training app Lumosity proof enough that somehow I'd made it through unscathed.

So in 2012, I threw my out-of-shape, 40-year-old ass into MMA workouts and got in better and better shape until eventually I was sparring. Despite concussions from my head slamming off the mat at Team Quest in Oregon, nearly being knocked out at Syndicate MMA in Las Vegas, a nasty head kick at Alliance MMA in Chula Vista, and brutal beatings by Fabricio Werdum and Renato Babalu at King's MMA in Huntington Beach, I planned to take a fight at 41 with absolutely nothing to gain by it.

It was October 2013, two days after talking to a matchmaker about finding me an opponent, and I'd just survived the advanced class at 10th Planet Jiu Jitsu Headquarters in Los Angeles where I'd been training a few weeks. I was exhausted and everything hurt, but the MMA coach talked me into sparring with his young fighters. It was ugly, but I hung in there for four rounds without having a heart attack.

TBI or CTE: What the Hell is Wrong with Me?

On the way to the car, my childhood friend and photographer, Brian Esquivel, asked if I'd read any articles about brain damage in football players and MMA fighters. As delicately as he could, he pointed out that I'd been getting the shit kicked out of me by athletes half my age.

That night I went to bed with a bad headache before I could do any research, but the next day I started digging. I discovered that simply knowing that getting hit in the head isn't healthy and understanding why it's not are two very different things.

The more I read about TBIs, the more I feared I had really screwed up. I was a reckless kid, experiencing my first serious concussion when I smacked my head on a schoolyard sprinkler when I was six or seven. It's impossible to count how many I've had since, but there have been plenty. In seven years of high school and college football, I'd lost consciousness six times. On top of that I'd had constant trauma playing defensive line like a ram, always striking helmet to helmet. While attempting an MMA career, I was knocked out twice. On another two occasions, my brain was rattled so badly that I completely lost at least 15 minutes of time, and there were a ridiculous number of instances when I left a gym with a moderate concussion. During the two years I boxed, I constantly slurred my words and reversed their order. Add a few motorcycle accidents and a 70-mph car collision, and it is amazing I can write my own name, let alone novels.

The cumulative brain trauma makes me a prime candidate for dementia and was likely responsible for my spotty memory.

How ironic that now I'd found my passion for writing, wanting to do it until the day I die, it looked like there was a good chance I'd spend some of those years unable to care for myself. Determined not to make my odds of dementia any worse, I promised Jen that I wouldn't take any more strikes to the head and would settle for the somewhat gentle art of jiu jitsu. I'm proud that I only broke that promise one time, a final light sparring at Lauzon

MMA in Massachusetts to drive home the lesson that I could no longer rationalize the risk.

Although I wasn't excessively worried about my brain health, I was concerned enough to implement some recommendations I found online. I began playing brain games on Lumosity and a couple of other platforms, my scores in the top percentiles assuring me I was fine.

The other big take-away from my limited research was the importance of exercise. Not only can regular exercise relieve stress, help with pain, and improve overall well-being, it's also good for the vascular system in your brain. Fortunately, I was motivated to continue training jiu jitsu and practicing yoga, feeling fit at the lightest weight I'd been since high school at 208 pounds.

In July 2015, I wrote to the Cleveland Clinic Lou Ruvo Center for Brain Health in Las Vegas. Several of the fighters I'd interviewed for *UTC* were participants in their Professional Fighter Brain Health study and highly recommended I try it since the study needed retired as well as current fighters.

The clinic sent me a stack of forms that I put off answering until an hour before my 10 o'clock appointment. It took me a while to tally up the number of matches, rounds, and concussions. Between boxing and MMA, I had 14 professional matches and a losing record, a sure sign I'd taken more damage than I had dealt.

I drove to the clinic, past the old boxing gym where I'd been battered around by heavyweights I'd watched fight on TV. I popped a cannabis-infused gummy, the only way I could function under stress. Plus, if the study wanted to assess how I functioned on a daily basis, this would give them the best look. I had another gummy in my pocket for the halfway point of the 4-hour test.

Waiting for the cannabis to kick in, I walked around the building, even though I was sweating from the heat. The building's design was uniquely beautiful, a metallic masterpiece designed by Frank Gehry, but its chaotic curves filled me with a sense of dread, an image of a twisted brain. The courtyard and surroundings were relaxing and peaceful though, and I was greeted by a friendly volunteer who guided me to reception.

The lobby was full; no doubt I was the youngest person by at least ten years. I wondered what types of brain degeneration the different individuals might be suffering. I told myself, *I don't fit in here. At least not yet.*

An assistant escorted me back and briefed me on the cognitive testing. I felt prepared because of Lumosity and scored above average on some tests, but my reaction time was only average. Next up, I stumbled through a couple of speech tests, but the assistant assured me I was doing fine.

The physical test was all about balance, and I was confident from doing a few months of yoga as rehab for a partially torn ACL. I felt solid standing with my feet together, hands on hips, eyes closed, but I just couldn't do it with my right leg raised. I tried again and again but couldn't hold the pose for more than a second. The assistant didn't say whether that indicated anything significant.

After a painless blood draw, I met with Dr. Charles Bernick, the associate medical director of the clinic and principal researcher of the study. At that time the study included about 400 current and 50 retired fighters.

I mentioned that I'd interviewed about the same number of MMA athletes from around the country and done a layman's assessment for noticeable signs of damage, especially with guys that had had long careers or taken a lot of abuse due to their fighting style. Overall, I'd detected very few indications of brain damage, even those with 40-plus fights under their belt, but I admitted that my brief and uneducated analysis was very limited since I didn't know the fighters before their careers and their self-assessments probably weren't very accurate. I believed many fighters might not notice subtle changes in behavior or ability and, if they did, they often attributed it simply to aging.

Dr. Bernick nodded and shared his similar impression of MMA fighters. He told me the repeated head trauma could lead to progressive neurological deficits, but it doesn't occur among all athletes. It's too early to guess what percentage of fighters might be affected, especially since the sport is so new and symptoms of permanent brain damage might not present for five years or more after the last trauma.

I couldn't help but wonder what my odds were. What did my tests indicate? What did my awful balance reveal?

We went over my history, Dr. Bernick taking note of everything, asking questions but skillfully avoiding my concerns. He continued the neurological examination by checking my reflexes, gait, and balance and had me follow his fingers with my eyes. He discussed the goals of the project and said he hoped to answer many of the questions I had.

The study's emphasis was on early identification of neurocognitive decline and prediction of long-term neurological consequences. They hoped to discover why, with similar levels of trauma, some fighters are more at risk for a decline in brain health. With the MRI I was about to undergo and the other tests I'd just finished, the researchers hoped to detect even the earliest and most subtle signs of brain injury. By repeating these tests several years in a row, they hoped to find biomarkers, or clinical indicators, that could predict cognitive decline and better understand the impact of each risk factor.

With so many fighters involved in the study and the massive amount of data acquired, it seems likely that the research team will reach their goals. The only problem is that, as to be expected with any volunteer longitudinal study, a number of participants won't complete the testing. The continued recording of data is where most answers will come from. Even if a fighter retires and no longer experiences head trauma, the comprehensive test results are invaluable.

I left the clinic relieved at my results and committed to the study. I encouraged other fighters to participate in the research and be more aware of their own brain health, to be proactive, doing whatever they can to postpone any decline.

I went back to the hotel, ate some more cannabis gummies and went gambling, putting my worries to rest.

Chapter Two

When I returned from the Cleveland Clinic, I fell back into my normal routines, taking care of my 2-year-old son and 7-year-old daughter while working on the writing of *Unlocking the Cage* and the release of *Twisted Reunion,* a collection of my short horror stories.

Following the example of the fighters I'd interviewed, I adopted a much healthier lifestyle and continued to practicing yoga and training jiu jitsu, getting my purple belt from Eddie Bravo at the end of 2016. This is one of the few accomplishments I'm proud of as it wasn't easy taking myself from being the joke of the gym, getting submitted by hundreds of different individuals each year, to holding my own against much younger athletes.

In addition to eating better and exercising to help with any potential brain issues, I got my first guitar, continued playing brain games on Lumosity, and began learning German. I also started a podcast called Unlocking with my yogi and good friend Anthony Johnson. Our cannabis-fueled talks on and off air proved to be a very cathartic form of therapy. Events that stood out for me that year were getting a tattoo on my right calf, reading *The Anatomy of Violence* by Adrian Raine, and having a powerful experience with N, N-Dimethyltryptamine (DMT), the spirit molecule.

2017 was a much more stressful year, with neck, back, and shoulder injuries keeping me from both yoga and jiu jitsu. I used the time off to use sensory deprivation tanks and tattoo my entire back with the illustration I intend to use for the cover of a fantasy trilogy I plotted out with my daughter. A chronic multitasker, I went into every tattoo session baked out of my mind so I could work on writing *Ain't No Messiah,* nearly passing out twice thanks to an unknown sensitivity to Vicodin.

TBI or CTE: What the Hell is Wrong with Me?

In October, I released *Unlocking the Cage*, which had great reviews but terrible sales, another contributor to the ongoing depression I kept bottled up. I tried not to worry about having something wrong with my brain, but the *Ultimate Yogi* video I practiced to three nights a week had a message that always hit me hard. It mentions the average life expectancy of an NFL player is around 56, about 20 years younger than that of the average male in the U.S. I wondered how much of that difference could be attributed to problems arising from brain health.

I began sharing articles and concern over traumatic brain injuries, and in November I received several messages from former football teammates and MMA fighters. Many of these men were silently dealing with brain damage, some participating in brain studies, a couple at the end of their rope.

It wasn't just about me anymore, something I could bury and forget about. Despite my promise that I wouldn't write any more nonfiction, I committed to explore chronic traumatic encephalopathy (CTE) and write a book on it. My goal would be to determine if I have CTE and then try absolutely everything I could to reverse it. I'd take the same approach as I did with *Unlocking the Cage*, travelling around the country for interviews, testing, and help. My focus would be on fighters and football players, investigating what we're up against and sharing ways to deal with our situation.

I amped up the recommended activities I'd been engaging in and added in cold-water therapy, spending 15 to 30 minutes in my pool that averaged about 54 degrees. Even though I was in the middle of writing a sequel to my novel *Brightside* and novella *Try Not to Die: In Brightside*, I promised myself the brain book would have top priority in 2018.

#

It was 10 a.m. on a Tuesday, a few weeks into the new year, and I was stoned in the backyard, discouraged by how little I'd worked on this book. I'd updated my list of experts I wanted to interview and therapies I'd like to attempt, but I had absolutely zero motivation to begin writing.

Perhaps my desire to help others wasn't as strong as I believed. This wouldn't be the first time I lost interest in something soon after the initial excitement. Coming up with ideas is often more fun than seeing them through, especially when it involves dwelling on brain damage every day.

One of the things I'd been hearing over and over in yoga was about having compassion for myself. True, I hadn't written much, but I had been keeping up with recommended activities, including the Wim Hof–inspired breathing and cold-water therapy that I was going to do the entire month. I'd committed to maintaining a well-balanced diet to help me feel better and regulate energy levels and was in the middle of a 4-week cleanse, a way for me to drop weight and get rid of the nagging worry that'd begun since one of my best friends had been diagnosed with cancer.

In addition to the activities, I also had been reading nonfiction. *The Brain that Changes Itself* by Dr. Norman Doidge is a fascinating book and largely responsible for my shifting out of hopelessness. Dr. Doidge looks at the new science of neuroplasticity and the people whose lives were transformed by it. The old thinking was that the brain could not be changed, only damaged, but this book shows just how powerful and adaptable our brains really are.

In the book, Dr. Doidge tells the story of stroke patients learning to move and speak again, how cognitive therapy can rewire brains, how plasticity can stop worries and obsessions, and how incredibly powerful our imagination and beliefs can be. By the end of the book, I understood our brains are much more resilient and adaptable than I'd thought. Even if I had done damage to my brain, there was hope I could fix it.

The next book I picked up had been buried in my to-read pile which sits beside my-probably-never-going-to-touch pile. I'd bought *Why We Sleep* by Matthew Walker, PhD back in November after spending time on the Concussion Legacy Foundation's website, where I'd read that one of the most important things you could do for your brain and overall health was get a full night's sleep. I'd seen that recommendation several places but never paid it any mind. They claimed that lack of adequate sleep could cause mental fogginess and headaches, as well as affect self-regulation and emotion. Getting seven to eight hours would lead to a healthier brain and could help rid the brain of the effects of CTE and other brain disorders.

I figured I'd only make it a few pages into the book before it put me to sleep, but I was dead wrong. The writing was excellent and engaging, the information scary. My teenage years and early adulthood were full of partying into the early morning. After that it was working graveyard shifts so I could train during the day. Once I had kids it only got worse: I was unable to start writing until after parenting duties were done and quit around one or two in the morning. I was one of those people who said they'd sleep when they were dead. There was no doubt I was hurting myself by not getting enough sleep, shortening my life by burning the candle on both ends.

Before I'd even gone halfway through the book, I realized it was one of the most important books I'd ever read. It completely changed the way I'd view sleep for the rest of my life. I purchased a Garmin watch to start tracking my sleep and I began driving my daughter to school, an 80-minute round-trip full of asshole drivers and inconsiderate parents. The added stress was worth it though because it enabled her to get an extra hour of needed sleep.

It was around this time that I finally watched The Joe Rogan Experience podcast #1056 recommended by my buddy Brian Esquivel, who had first warned me about brain damage. I didn't want to watch it because, although I love Joe Rogan and have seen his live stand-up routine close to a dozen times, I didn't want to spend an hour and a half listening to some military guy and a doctor.

In the episode, Andrew Marr, a former special forces Green Beret, went into detail about how his life derailed and he could find no explanation or relief until he discovered Dr. Mark Gordon, the owner of Millennium Neuro Regenerative Centers, and a worldwide leader in antiaging medicine (interventional endocrinology).

On the podcast, Dr. Gordon described what happens when a traumatic brain injury occurs and dispelled lots of the myths surrounding them. Most people assume an individual needs to be knocked unconscious or have a very significant blow to the head in order to have a TBI, but Dr. Gordon explained the process could be started more easily, even by a minor car accident or a ride on a roller coaster. Once the injury occurs, the brain becomes inflamed, and this inflammation expands and disrupts the brain's ability to self-regulate hormones.

Dr. Gordon explained that so many symptoms of post-traumatic stress disorder (PTSD) and TBIs overlap such as depression, anxiety, irritability, cognitive deficits, insomnia, and fatigue. In Dr. Gordon's opinion, PTSD is a manifestation of a TBI. Head injuries are often forgotten but commonly identified during detailed patient histories. His approach is to treat patients with hormone replacement therapy to reduce the inflammation in the brain that has compromised functioning resulting from the injury. He claimed to have turned around the lives of about 1,500 military personnel.

Although I didn't believe I needed the protocol, I talked it over with my wife and we agreed the cost of the program would be worth trying. Even if it didn't do anything for me, I could write about it in this book. I contacted Dr. Gordon's office and found that their normal waiting time had jumped from one week to eight weeks due to a flood of requests from listeners to the Rogan podcast.

While waiting to be admitted to Dr. Gordon's practice, I continued working on my fiction and keeping my cool, spending most of my day relatively high on cannabis, only using sativas because they helped me with focus and creativity.

In February, I began a two-month break from social media just as the *Unlocking the Cage* hardcover released. As an independent author, it is crucial that I maintain an active social media presence, but instead of launching a huge marketing push I closed shop, a sure sign that I was sabotaging myself.

My right shoulder had become such a problem that it was wrecking my sleep, and in April I had my first cortisone injection so I could function. The very next week, I had my blood drawn for Dr. Gordon and then headed to Vegas for another visit to the Cleveland Clinic, depressed because I wouldn't be able to train jiu jitsu with my friends and scared at what I might discover about my brain.

Chapter Three

Vegas is always an interesting place for me to visit. It's a reminder of a reckless life full of drugs, alcohol, gambling, a failed marriage, and so very little sleep while I worked the graveyard shift as a correctional officer at a prison and again as a juvenile probation officer. My diet back then had been atrocious and my blood pressure so high that I'd been put on medication out of fear I was going to have a stroke.

I was more nervous for this visit to the Cleveland Clinic because in addition to undergoing another batch of testing, I'd arranged an interview with Dr. Bernick so we could discuss CTE and any changes in me. I was also worried about the headache I hadn't been able to kick for the past week, my poor sleep, impaired judgment, increased anger, and anxiety attacks.

Just as I had on my first visit, I popped a cannabis gummy and went through the testing. I ate another one before the MRI and sitting down with Dr. Bernick afterward to go over my questions and concerns.

Overall, I felt pretty good, my testing still high and no significant changes showing on the MRI. Bernick helped me realize that the lack of exercise and added stress combined with poor sleep was much more likely the cause of my headache and current symptoms than CTE.

Although I'd read up on chronic traumatic encephalopathy, I asked Dr. Bernick to explain what it was so I could better understand it.

"So we really don't know that much about it at the moment," he said, not a very reassuring start to the conversation. "It is a progressive disease of the brain associated with repetitive head trauma. The problem is most of what we know, what has come out from literature, is that everything's coming out from the Brain Bank and nearly everyone in the Brain Bank has CTE."

Defined pathologically, CTE is the presence of the protein tau in characteristic locations of the brain and around blood vessels, according to Dr. Bernick. He said, "If you have that, it's called CTE. And that's very common if you have had a lot of head trauma. That's why ninety-nine out of one hundred pro football players have it."

While some will suffer from the progressive disease where cells degenerate, tau spreads and progressive dementia develops, others who have had injury to the brain from repeated head trauma seem able to control and manage it. Others have a lot of head trauma and see no symptoms.

Dr. Bernick said one of the biggest problems with our understanding of this disease is that there is no method to predict or diagnose in a living person which of these courses they're going to take unless you follow them over time. "That's where lots of the research is going, to diagnose those developing it, and hopefully find ways to intervene. In other diseases we learn from animals, but we don't have a good animal model that replicates the human."

Not knowing the correct term, I asked if tau was poisonous or toxic. "Is it the tau that causes the degeneration?"

"Nobody knows if it's the marker of injury or it injures cells itself," Dr. Bernick said. "Tau is a protein that's important in the maintenance of the structure of the brain cell fiber, and we know those fibers are the ones susceptible to injury from head trauma. Because the brain is squished around, the fibers are stretched and injured, so it's not surprising that tau gets malformed or misshaped and can accumulate. The question is if it spreads and injures other cells."

What really separates the tau found in CTE from the tau in Alzheimer's is location. "You see it around blood vessels, and at the depths of the sulci, so it's very superficial in the brain and it can be scattered about. In Alzheimer's the tau starts in the temporal lobe and moves from there. With CTE it is more diffuse and scattered."

I asked Dr. Bernick what approaches he thought might be worthwhile. The first theory he mentioned was targeting the chronic inflammation in the brain, which I was glad to hear since I was only weeks away from trying this with Dr. Gordon's protocol.

He also mentioned that drugs that remove tau and amyloids seem promising, as well as those that help stabilize nerve cell membranes. He said, "There could be a lot of different strategies and drugs available, just at the moment we don't have any evidence that these strategies work."

When asked what advice he'd pass on to fighters or anyone worried about brain health, he said, "Active fighters need to change their training, just like the NFL has done. Without question the most significant factor in determining CTE or any of these conditions, is the amount of exposure you have. Going all out in sparring is not a great idea. If you get your bell rung you need to take time off. So if there is inflammation you need to let it settle down. If you've had a concussion it's going to be easier to cause another one. People just have to be smart. Smart on training, how many fights they have a year, so that's how active fighters can prolong their career and reduce the chance of long-term effects."

For fighters who have retired, he said the procedure is to use what is already known about brain health. Two of the biggest factors that have helped the brain in other diseases are adequate sleep and aerobic exercise, 40 minutes, four to five days a week, with a heartrate at 70 percent.

Dr. Bernick said that diet may be important, supplements not so much. He stressed the importance of getting nutrients from natural sources, such as vegetables, berries, dry fruit, and fish.

He also recommended staying away from things like alcohol and marijuana that may not help the cause. I had no comment.

TBI or CTE: What the Hell is Wrong with Me?

Dr. Bernick stressed the power of the brain and its plasticity. He said keeping active, training the brain, and mindfulness techniques are huge and can help individuals deal with depression and other symptoms.

I asked Dr. Bernick his thoughts on the appropriate age to play contact sports and whether recent rule changes have made sports much safer. Although he is glad to see advancements in protecting fighters and players, he pointed out that so much of it rests on individuals admitting they'd had a concussion. "I assume if you don't play or fight, someone else is going to get your position. There's an incentive to not tell anyone about your concussion."

I'd experienced that firsthand, rarely telling coaches of concussions for fear I'd be benched, not to mention I often looked at it as a weakness.

As for the age, Dr. Bernick said, "This is kind of tricky. In football, studies suggest that those who start younger did a little worse with the brain, same with fighters. The brain is developing at this time, so it probably makes sense to hold off any contact sports until you've gone through teen years."

The professional fighter study was going on its seventh year and is very promising, but Dr. Bernick reminded me that CTE, Alzheimer's and such are diseases that evolve over decades so they are very hard to track. He stressed how important it is to intervene early and that the recovery must be part of your lifestyle.

I thanked Dr. Bernick for his time and for the wonderful work he'd dedicated his life to. I promised I'd be back in a year for another follow-up.

Chapter Four

A few weeks after returning from the Cleveland Clinic, I was on a Skype conference call with Dr. Alison Gordon, Dr. Mark Gordon's daughter, a naturopathic doctor and the cofounder of LIVV Natural Health in San Diego.

Before we went over my history, Dr. Alison gave me a quick rundown on the Millennium Neuro Regenerative Centers and its goals. She explained that when we suffer an injury, whether knockout, blast wave, repetitive gunfire, car accident, or a simple blow to the head, two things happen. First is the immediate structural damage that causes tearing of long nerves and microvascular structures. The second follows immediately with biochemical reactions that cause inflammation in the brain.

This inflammation continues to evolve over time and expands the damage to other areas of the brain, overwhelming its ability to defend itself. Oxidative stress with free radical damage alters important biochemical processes, and we find it difficult to regulate cognitive and behavioral functions. Our memory and ability to learn go down as our anger, depression, and irritability increase. It also causes insomnia, fatigue, headaches, diminished libido, disorientation, and alcohol and drug abuse.

As the inflammation increases, the brain's ability to produce and regulate hormones goes down. The loss of neurosteroids, such as progesterone, testosterone and a dozen others, makes the ability to recover very difficult.

Essentially, TBIs can cause premature aging, and it is estimated that there are close to five million people walking around with the residual effects from them, with two million new cases each year. Most treatments simply mask the symptoms, but at Millennium they focus on reducing the inflammation in the brain and regulating these hormones.

TBI or CTE: What the Hell is Wrong with Me?

After the overview, we went over my history, symptoms, questions, concerns, and hopes. Then we dove into my blood chemistry, which she said was consistent with someone who has had multiple TBIs.

Dr. Alison also reminded me that she and her colleagues aren't like other doctors who disregard low or high numbers simply because they fall within the reference range. For example, normal values of pregnenolone for people over 18 years range between 33 and 248 ng/dL. If my results came back at 40, many doctors would say it wasn't an issue because I was within the acceptable range. At Millennium they bring patients to the median number or higher which generally results in much better functioning.

As for my specifics, here are the items that were not ideal and what they influence:

DHEA-S, the precursor to testosterone and estrogens, was low-normal. DHEA-S helps protect the heart, reduce inflammation in the brain, increase myelin production, increase growth hormone (GH) and mood elevation.

Free testosterone was low-normal. This form of testosterone is the most important as it is the form that gets into cells and into the brain. In males, testosterone is associated with mental functioning, energy level, libido, sense of well-being, learning, memory, body fat and muscle proportions, cholesterol levels, bone density, and tissue healing.

Progesterone was low-normal. This hormone's active metabolite, allopregnenolone, is neuroprotective, neuroregenrative, and improves nerve-to-nerve communication at the synapse. The hormone also removes free radicals that cause damage and increases the production of gamma-aminobutyric acid (GABA), which has a calming effect.

The neuroprotective pregnenolone was low-normal. Interruption in this hormone will lead to a diminution in many other hormones.

Both follicle-stimulating hormone (FSH) and luteinizing hormone (LH), which reflect the body's ability to make testosterone from the testes, were low-normal.

Prolactin, a marker for hypothalamic-pituitary functioning, was low-normal. This also contributes to lower testosterone.

Vitamin D was extremely low. It is a marker of good bone development, repair, and health. Research is showing it can also decrease depression, dementia, Alzheimer's, and cancer; protects the heart; stimulates the immune system; reduces inflammation; and improves fine muscles and bone density in addition to having many other benefits.

To correct the imbalances and achieve optimal levels, Dr. Gordon prescribed Clomid, a pill taken every three days that helps the testes produce more testosterone. The other supplements I was directed to take were all over the counter: UltraNutrient, DHEA, Pregnenolone, Ultra B-Complex with PQQ, Vitamin D3 10,000 IU, NAC 900, and Ultra Synergist E.

I was also given a bottle of Dr. Mark Gordon's Clear Mind and Energy, which I hoped could replace my morning caffeine. My caffeine consumption was very high and dangerous for someone who didn't work out regularly but was very active on training days.

The other thing I went over with Dr. Alison was my use of cannabis, which made complete sense to her after seeing my bloodwork. Although she did not have a problem with patients consuming cannabis, she said I should be aware that my use would probably go down once I began the protocol. I didn't believe her but said I would keep an eye on it.

While I waited for the supplements to arrive, I returned to my normal routine, which also included weekly therapist visits. As part of this book, I had wanted to find a mental health professional who could assess me and my personality and then monitor how I responded to the different types of treatments I would attempt. Dr. Norman Doidge's book had engrained in me that cognitive therapy could rewire the brain. Perhaps it could also help me figure out why I've always been so dark and spent most of my life hating myself. But the real reason I finally began seeing someone was that my marriage needed it. Over the last few years, my wife and I had become roommates, partners raising our kids. After a frustrating search and a handful of psychologists who wouldn't return calls, I connected with Mark Harris from Harris Marriage and Family Therapy in La Habra.

Prior to my session with Mark, I'd only been to therapy as an adult twice, both visits in Vegas when that marriage was crumbling. Although I didn't stick with that therapist, he made me realize I was a perfectionist and would never be happy unless that changed. That understanding has been huge, so I went into this new therapy with a healthy mindset.

Before we got into much of anything else, Mark pointed out all the ways in which I'd been failing as a husband. Not intentionally failing, but still failing. He had me read *The Female Brain* by neuropsychiatrist Louann Brizendine and helped me understand what it is that women need. It also pointed out how my attempts to solve my wife's problems so she wouldn't feel pain were actually causing more pain by not validating her feelings, something Jen said over and over with me denying it every time.

I took Mark's advice and began making changes and seeing improvement in our relationship, but I was still dealing with all the other issues, covering them up with excessive cannabis use and my mind flying on caffeine. We dug into my childhood, and I began to see the source of lots of my darkness and anger; but it didn't make anything go away. I assumed it was going to take a while.

As a fun little exercise to see how screwed up I was, Mark had me take the Millon Clinical Multiaxial Inventory – III test. Here are the items that I scored high on:

Avoidant – 71

Narcissistic – 67
Antisocial – 79
Sadistic – 69
Alcohol Dependence – 75
Drug Dependence – 81

The only reason the alcohol dependence ranked so high was because of the questions asking about past behavior; I was most definitely a heavy drinker from 15 to 35 years old. Mark also had me do an interesting self-assessment of my fears and reactions.

For those of you who've always dreamed of upsetting me, here are my top fears and triggers:

Rejection: I'm not necessary; I feel unwanted.

Disconnected: Emotionally detached or separated.

Like a failure: Not successful at being a husband, father, author. I'm not good enough.

Coming in right behind them were —

Defective: Something's wrong with me. I'm the problem.

Inadequate: I'm not capable or competent.

Invalidated: Who I am, what I think, what I do, and how I feel are not valued.

Unloved: The other person doesn't care about me.

Worthless: I am useless. I have no value to the other person.

Now here's how I'm going to react if you do trigger me. Don't say you weren't warned. My worst reactions and defenses are —

Passive-Aggressive: I display negative emotions in passive ways, such as becoming stubborn.

Escalation: My emotions spiral out of control. I argue, raise my voice, and fly into a rage.

Rationalization: I attribute my behavior to credible motives.

Next up, but nearly just as high, were —
Indifference: I am cold and show no concern.
Minimization: The other person is overreacting to an issue. I downplay it.
Sarcasm: I use negative humor, hurtful words, or demeaning statements.
Numbing out: I become devoid of emotion or have no regard for others' emotions.
Acting Out: I engage in negative behaviors such as alcohol and drug abuse, overeating.
Anger and Rage: I display strong feelings of displeasure and have uncontrolled emotions.
Withdrawal: I avoid others or alienate myself without resolution.
Blaming: I place the responsibility on others and I don't accept fault.
Invalidation: I devalue the other person and their thoughts, feelings, and actions.
Defensiveness: I defend myself before listening to the argument.

Essentially, I'm a scared little boy who lashes out at others. In my brain journal I wrote that therapy had seemed to reduce my overall anger and anxiety, but it was still there.

The supplements came from Dr. Alison's office the second week of June, and within a few days of being on the protocol I found myself using less and less cannabis, noting that it made me feel too anxious. Every day I cut back a little more, trying to find the sweet spot, using about half of my former amount at the two-week mark.

About that same time, I found myself crying in the backyard, not because anything was wrong but because I felt no sense of ill ease. This was the first time I'd ever realized just how terrible my symptoms had been. Not having the weight of the incredibly high levels of anger, depression, and irritability was stunning. After another two weeks on the protocol, I felt as if I were in the best emotional place I'd ever been with a mental clarity I'd been lacking.

Summer was uneventful, largely thanks to a shoulder injury keeping me out of competition and training. Despite the injury, my overall mood was much better. I had however regained my cannabis tolerance and was overindulging to mask symptoms.

With the start of the school year, I began attending classes at Downey Yoga to help my physical and mental well-being, a much-needed stress release. In October, we redid my bloodwork for Dr. Alison and saw that all my levels had improved over the six months, but my free testosterone and IGF-1 were still low-normal. We were on the right track and I did feel much better.

The other thing I did in October was go sober, sticking with it for a full 40 days despite my intention to only do 30. At first not having any cannabis was rough, on both me and my family, but by the end I felt like I could live without it if I had to.

In November I did a stem cell injection for my shoulder, and the next month I released the advance copies of my latest novel, *Ain't No Messiah*. Life was good and I felt like I was successfully managing my work and family.

With regular yoga and biweekly therapy sessions, my life felt back on track. With things running smoothly, I focused on my physical health and writing my *Brightside* sequels, thoughts of the brain book pushed to the side.

Then one day in April while flipping through Facebook, I discovered that Michael Poorman, a former teammate from Brown University, was in a losing battle against leukemia. Michael had written to me a year and a half earlier to disclose he'd been diagnosed with CTE symptoms and was a participant in the Legacy

TBI or CTE: What the Hell is Wrong with Me?

study at the Mayo Clinic. Never one to mince words, he said, "My brain is fucked."

Michael's message along with those of a few other offensive linemen suffering with brain issues led me to start this book. I'd never followed up with him on it, but now that he was dying, I wanted to do anything I could to at least let him know I was thinking of him. I offered to help him write a story that he could give to friends and family at a celebration of life party Michael had planned in July.

A few weeks later, we finally talked on the phone. I was at the park playing with my son, and Michael explained his situation and just how bad his brain problems had been. It was a sobering talk, and I shared how inspired I was by the way he was living his life and dealing with impending death. When I asked him if he'd like to be in this book, he said he would but only if he agreed with the approach I'd be taking with it. After I told him my angle, he said he'd love to help any way he could and invited me up to Astoria, Oregon, to spend a few days with him and his family. When I got off the phone, I was looking at summer and my son in a whole different light.

Chapter Five

Over the past decade, I'd been to Oregon seven times. Two of the trips were with my family in the last year in the hope we might relocate there and another two visits when I was working on *Unlocking the Cage*. The first three visits were to see my writing mentor, Tom Spanbauer, and his partner, Sage Ricci, who tattooed the inside of my right bicep.

In 2009, on the second of those trips to visit Tom and Sage, Michael Poorman, who was living in Battle Ground, Washington, took me fishing on the Columbia River. I don't remember much about the day besides the beauty and Michael being very friendly, open, and straightforward. I'd only known him for 1 year at Brown, but my impression of him was as someone who had gone out of his way to make me feel welcome and part of the football team. As a larger-than-life Oregonian who grew up on a survivalist compound, Michael could spot an outsider and knew what it was like to feel a little different.

Unlike normal trips where I try to squeeze in training and writing, this one was dedicated to Michael. If I knew my days were numbered, I'm not sure I'd be so kind with my time and spend it talking to an old acquaintance about a painful subject.

So I didn't feel like a complete stranger, I ran through Michael's life on Facebook, memorized the names of his wife and kids. Even though I had GPS and Michael gave me detailed instructions to get to his in-laws in Astoria where he and his family were staying for the month, I pulled up to the wrong house. Fortunately, a friendly face popped out a second-story window. The blond teenager asked if I was looking for her father and pointed out the beautiful Victorian house across the street.

Michael greeted me, filling the doorway at 6'5 and 250 pounds. Although he would later show me photos to prove how much muscle he had lost, had he not told me about the cancer, I never would've guessed.

After a quick introduction to Sara, his beautiful wife of 14 years, the three of us headed to lunch with Sara behind the wheel. Michael had recommended that I interview Sara as she was the one who had done all the research on CTE and his cancer and would be able to provide me with an alternative perspective. I was grateful she was able and willing to join us.

Having just come from the gym, Sara was hoping for a nice salad, which sounded perfect to me, but Michael had his heart set on taking me to his favorite pub. She explained they didn't have good salads there, but Michael said they had his favorite beer and he wanted me to experience the view of the river. Although I sensed a little irritation on both ends, Sara remained calm and let it go.

It was beautiful outside on the dock, but also chilly. After a few minutes of watching me shiver in my T-shirt, Michael walked around the table and put his jacket around my shoulders. Had it been any other male, I probably would have refused, but I thanked him and we got in some small talk about our families while figuring what to order.

When the food arrived, we dug into the issue. When was the first time they realized there might be something wrong with Michael's brain?

There was no hesitation on either end. It was 2013, a year after they'd returned from a two-year stay in Australia. They were at a party when Sara noticed Michael's behavior was a little odd. At first, she attributed it to alcohol, but it got worse, Michael becoming agitated and delirious, the police being called.

By the time the police arrived, Sara and others were afraid Michael may have had a stroke. He was taken away in an ambulance to the hospital, where the doctors realized something was going on with his brain and ordered an MRI.

The neurologist called it a dissociative episode, which is an involuntary escape from reality. The doctor compared the MRI of Michael's brain to that of a 75-year-old with a deeply ridged frontal lobe very similar to Michael's.

We continued lunch and I asked a few questions, just so I would be able to formulate more for the real interview the following morning, which I would record because, as Michael could relate to, my memory was awful.

Throughout the lunch, Sara was very aware of our surroundings and seemed a little on edge, like she was just waiting for something bad to happen. The more they described how Michael's CTE could be set off, the more I understood she was protecting Michael, herself, and the others around us.

Back at the house, Michael and I pulled chairs up to the firepit while Sara, a brilliant mechanical engineer, built the fire. Whether she was around us or inside the house, Michael couldn't stop praising Sara and bragging about how smart she is. He was incredibly proud of her, both of us feeling that we got the much better deal in our marriages.

Over pizza and beer, Michael and I did a lot of catching up, Michael telling me stories about Brown that we both thought I should have remembered. The afternoon spilled into the evening, our conversation zipping all over the place, as we watched his son Mateo play with his cousin on the front lawn while Michael and I took turns throwing balls to their adorable little dog, Boris. I checked my phone and was shocked to see it was still light out at nine o'clock, time for both of us to get some rest.

I returned to the house the next morning to catch Michael at his best, his Adderall kicking in, which would help him with focus. Not wanting to waste any of their time or energy, I set up my recorder in a quiet room where there wouldn't be any distractions. Michael and Sara joined me, and we got started with a recap of

TBI or CTE: What the Hell is Wrong with Me?

Michael's history, specifically looking for early signs of head trauma since it seems those injuries do the most damage.

The earliest concussion Michael could remember was in elementary school. To impress a girl, Michael tried to do a flip on the monkey bars, the back of his head slamming down on the asphalt, knocking him unconscious and leaving him with three stitches.

Although he hadn't thought much of it when the subject came up the day before, I asked Michael about his boxing. He began Golden Gloves at six, with his first bout at seven. He continued amateur boxing for the next seven years and for two more while at Brown. Altogether he had 63 bouts, even one against a young Michael Grant, who would go on to become the world heavyweight title challenger.

When asked if he thought the boxing might have had any effect on his brain damage, Michael said no; he always wore headgear.

I didn't want to burst his bubble, but I told him my understanding was that headgear doesn't do shit for our brain. It provides a false sense of security and does very little to lessen the force of the blow. Headgear is great for preventing lacerations, but two of my worst concussions occurred while wearing top-of-the-line headgear, not to mention the countless mild ones.

Michael also pointed out that he had never been knocked out in boxing.

Having five professional boxing bouts under my belt and plenty of sparring, I knew it was common to go down but remain conscious. I asked him if that had ever happened to him.

"Oh yeah. I definitely got knocked on my ass and had my legs give out."

We left boxing alone and went on to football. Michael started tackle football in sixth grade and had his first concussion from it the following year and had to sit out practice for two days. In ninth grade, he had another one and was told to shake it off. Any time he would have headaches throughout his football career, he was careful not to use his head, something he managed to do quite well as he was one of the biggest kids on the field.

Michael's time at Brown University was when things grew more serious. His first concussion only caused him to miss one practice. The second one knocked Michael out for a few seconds and he was taken for a CT scan, which showed three blood spots. Ten days later the scan was clean, and Michael returned to the field. He felt his third concussion was relatively mild, leaving him disoriented as he stumbled to the wrong huddle.

I reminded Michael that a concussion is not what we were taught to believe. What about having his bell rung, getting a dinger, feeling woozy after a big hit?

He said, "Those happened all the time. That was part of the game."

I asked, "Were there any thoughts about future damage? Did you consider not playing anymore out of fear?"

Michael shook his head. "Back then we all knew Muhammed Ali was fucked up and stuttering, but that was understandable. Getting punched like that could cause problems, but there was no danger from football."

Although Michael had been in a handful of scuffles off the field, he didn't believe those resulted in any concussions. The same went for the one car accident 25 years ago when he'd hit his head on the steering wheel.

I wasn't sure if it might have contributed to his CTE, but I'd been reading how repetitive gunfire could cause TBIs. Knowing he was a gun fanatic, I asked, "Have you done a lot of shooting?"

"Fuck yeah, dude. At my bachelor party we did seven thousand rounds with machine guns. Hell, we did fifteen hundred rounds the weekend before last. There was a time I was shooting every week. We had a gun range in my basement. I grew up on a survivalist compound. Guns were definitely part of the equation."

There was another factor that might have played a role, but I didn't bring it up. As a very successful businessman, Michael had constantly been flying around the country. Jet lag can greatly affect sleep and the brain, but it was time to move on.

"So when did the first signs begin? Was there anything prior to the dissociative episode in 2013?"

Sara said, "Looking back, I'd say it first started kicking in when we came back from Australia in 2012. It crept up over time. There were little shifts in his personality."

After the dissociative episode and brain scan, Michael was diagnosed with Stage 2 CTE symptoms and sundowners, which is a neurological phenomenon associated with increased confusion and restlessness in patients with a form of dementia that typically gets worse as the day progresses.

I wondered if he had any of the warning signs. "Did you have headaches prior?"

"I never got a lot of headaches," Michael said. But he also realized that for a couple of years leading up to the episode he'd been taking muscle relaxers for his back and enough drugs for other conditions that might have masked headaches.

"How was your memory before all this?"

He said his memory was great until his mid-20s when he stopped being able to remember people's names. Understanding how important that was in the business world, Michael researched ways to improve his ability and began writing mental stories about people, often wowing others with the things he remembered about them.

Sara said, "His short-term memory, especially when he's in an agitated state, he won't remember at all or it will be really spotty."

I asked what some of his other issues were.

Michael said, "On a scale of one to ten, a two event happens, your emotional reaction should be a two, but sometimes I'll respond at a nine."

I asked if he'd been like that before, and he said no, not really.

Sara said, "Michael has always been a big, demonstrative guy and has a big personality, type A and assertive. Having that personality type was an asset when well-executed in life and his career field." However, once the CTE came into play, Sara said that personality type wound up working against him and became a liability.

"I became a director for a multibillion-dollar software company," Michael said. "I took two companies public. I built a hell of a career and if it wasn't for CTE I'd probably be a CEO somewhere."

As Michael progressed in his career, the responsibilities became greater, as did the stakes. Due to his sundowners, Michael had to modify his schedule, taking breakfast meetings instead of dinners or happy hours. If he was going to get a box to entertain clients at Boston Garden or Staples Center, he'd show up for the game but leave by first period.

I asked if that was just a precaution against the rare chance he'd have an outburst or inappropriate reaction.

He shook his head. "More often than not, it was going to happen."

Sara said, "We went through many years of keeping it quiet and creating coping mechanisms so Michael's business constituents wouldn't find out. There was a fear of him being devalued or compromising his career."

They also didn't tell family or friends for a long time, only revealing it to his closest friends if they were going to be out with Michael at night. He said, "This is not a badge of honor. It's something people don't understand.

TBI or CTE: What the Hell is Wrong with Me?

"CTE is fucking embarrassing. It's a loss of control. When I start having my CTE outbursts, I'd be embarrassed but I wish Sara could film it. It's like I'm having an out of body experience because it's like half my mind realizes that what I'm doing is absurd but half my mind is like a dog on the bone, I am right, you are wrong, fuck you. I start raising my voice and yelling. Two minutes into the outburst, the logical side of my brain that's still there says, dude, why are you even fucking arguing, do you even know what you're arguing about right now."

He said, "After one of my episodes, I just feel like a bag of shit. I'm full of shame and guilt. I feel out of control, that I'm not in control of my own faculties. I feel embarrassed. I don't want to say I feel depressed. If I didn't know why I was having these experiences, I would probably feel really depressed.

"Sara says it's like a dog crashing in the mirror, like I'm fighting with myself. It makes me feel like a shitty dad. Makes me feel like it created separation between Sara and I."

I asked, "Can you forgive yourself? Can you see it's not really you?"

"I absolutely forgive myself. First thing I do is make an amend. I apologize to my family and say I'm really sorry and I love you. I've never laid a hand on my wife or kids. I never have. I guess I scare the fuck out of them with yelling."

I hated having to ask, "Are you afraid you might be a danger to them at some point?"

"I would hope not. Honestly, Mark, I would commit suicide before I did that. If it progressed to that point, I'd pull a Junior Seau and put a shotgun on my heart."

We paused for a bathroom break and I confided with Sara just how guilty I felt, not only because I was okay and Michael wasn't, but also because I was looking for any signs that would show why he developed much worse CTE symptoms than I had. Michael and I shared many of the same traits, both being bigger men with shaved heads, goatees, and plenty of tattoos. Not to mention all the emotional similarities and struggles with anger, addiction, and narcissism. It was difficult for me not to look at him and fear that is what my future holds.

Sara assured me that that was a normal reaction and that she completely understood. Her hope was that by sharing their story, they could help others, including me, see their symptoms and come up with coping strategies.

Back in the room, guessing I knew the answer, I asked Michael, "Would you do it all again?"

"I've always been outcome oriented," Michael said. "I would not have gotten into Brown University had I not played football. It's a great conversation starter, definitely opened doors for me in business. I look at where I am right now with family, financially, and all that and absolutely I would do it again. If you asked me if I would want my son to do it, I would say no."

Sara was stunned and asked him if he was serious. "At our current crossroads you would do it again?"

"Well, my cancer's not from football."

"Yes, but fighting your cancer's been affected by football."

The cancer had only been discovered a few months earlier when Michael went to the doctor for another issue. A few days later, driving home from work, he received a phone call from his doctor telling him to go immediately to the emergency room, that his immune system was gone. Forty-two hours later, Michael was diagnosed with acute myeloid leukemia and undergoing chemotherapy.

Sara said, "Around the time most people get chemo brain, forgetful, tired, agitated, Michael started doing that, but it very quickly turned a corner and went beyond chemo brain. Agitation became where they needed to sedate him. The confusion became an inability to advocate for himself. The delirium became full-blown hallucinations, a fear of being attacked, them versus us, always some kind of war going on. At that point they brought in neurology and psychiatry. They moved him to a quieter room with consolidated care to lower stimulation in the environment."

Michael's oncologist hadn't even heard about CTE when Sara brought it up as a possible reason for her husband's extreme reaction to chemo. They contacted Boston University, where Michael is part of the LEGEND (Longitudinal Examination to Gather Evidence of Neurodegenerative Disease) study. Since Michael is the first person in the study fighting a blood cancer, the Boston University researchers didn't have any answers but understood Michael's fear that he would lose his mind in the process of trying to survive the cancer.

Chemo was stopped and Sara said, "It took the course of several weeks for him to have better cognition."

Doctors couldn't tell if the chemo/CTE mix had caused irreversible damage, but Michael said, "Post chemo it takes less to set me off. My CTE has definitely progressed and I now have a slight tremor in my left hand."

Michael said, "I'm a math guy. At the most simple level, I did not have the genetic markers for success. There are five specific markers. If you have those, they have treatments with a 97 percent rate for a five-year-outcome. With my genetic markers I had less than a 20 percent chance of a five-year-outcome and that's with reinduction and five more rounds of chemo, basically being chained to a hospital bed for seven to ten months. With the probability that I would be a vegetable. I looked at it doing two months of positive stuff. I don't want my kids to see me that way. I want my kids to remember a gentle giant that might get pissed off every now and then. A big strong guy. I just did not want to end up an animal or less than an animal.

"If I had the genetic markers, even with the CTE I would have done it, but the math just wouldn't work."

Sara said, "This is a one-way street and I know where it's going, but part of me just wants to throw him over my shoulder and carry him back to Mayo and say pump him full of poison so there's a small chance. It's selfish. I've entertained the idea because at least he'll be alive even if he has very diminished capacity and tremors.

"I can very quickly take away that selfish thought I'm having and I can understand Michael's dignity as a human being. That's not a dignified way to live for him. I can honor his choice, but it's a day-to-day struggle because I know I wield the power potentially that if I pushed him hard enough, I could get him to go in there and submit to treatment and that's tough."

Michael said, "Maybe they can keep me breathing and my heart beating for another year, but I'm not alive. The physical acts that it took to cause that brain damage, those were not the acts of cowardly men. Those were not the acts of beta men. Those were the acts of alpha males, courageous men. How guys like that live their life and the mental image they have of themselves, that diminished capacity sucks.

"People are afraid of death," Michael said. "I'm a Christian. If Heaven is real, I know where I'm going. I have a lot of sadness about not experiencing weddings, anniversaries, and things like that. There is sadness there. Instead of a fear of death, there is a fear of being a burden on someone else, diminished capacity."

After interviewing their daughter, O'Shen, I said my goodbyes and returned to the hotel, spending much of that night and the next morning in tears, not sure I was up for this journey. But I refocused and headed home to my family, determined to do whatever I could to prevent the slide. I'd be back in six weeks with my wife for Michael's celebration of life party.

Chapter Six

I'm back on a plane to Oregon, my wife reading a book beside me. Perhaps I don't have everything squared away like I had hoped, but I'm in a much better place now than when I wrote the prologue last week. A big part of the reason for that was the conversation I'd just had with Dr. Alison Gordon to discuss my blood work.

After a year on the Millennium Neuro Regenerative Centers' protocol, my blood chemistry is nearly where we want it. When I confided in Dr. Alison that I was worried about emotional instability and anger issues, she assured me that what I was experiencing was normal considering all the circumstances.

The main problem she pointed out was that I had not been exercising. Unlike the last few years when I was regularly training jiu jitsu and practicing yoga, I had been largely sedentary outside of the limited physical therapy I'd been doing for various injuries.

In addition to not having the physical outlet for emotional stability, she also pointed out that I was stressed from not having much time to write during summers and that I was researching a disturbing subject that takes me back to dark times. My responses to stress had been engrained and would have to be reexamined if I didn't want to continue having the same reactions.

She said that the engrained stress response also went for my excess caffeine and cannabis consumption. "We reach for the things that bring us calm," she told me. She suggested that I not consume cannabis 1 week each month to reset my levels and tolerance.

I asked, "What if I do one day off every couple days? Wouldn't that work the same?"

Her answer was, "How about seven days in a row? You can do it."

And to help me get my caffeine consumption in check she went over some of the dangers associated with heavy use such as acidic stomach and overstimulation of the adrenals, which could shut them off.

Knowing my fear that I would develop CTE, Dr. Alison recommended I reread *The Biology of Belief*, which my acupuncturist had suggested a few days before. The first time I read that book was several years prior to my brain research and it helped me become aware of just how powerful our beliefs are. Although I don't think positive thinking would stop CTE from advancing, I accepted that negative and fear-based beliefs would only cause more physical and emotional problems. I had to get my head straight and think positively as my wife had been encouraging me to do.

One of the best things Dr. Alison said was that health and wellness are a lifelong journey. You can't just take a pill and expect everything to be better. That was exactly what I needed to hear. I could no longer tell myself that if I take all my vitamins and supplements, everything will be all good.

Although I didn't dig *The Biology of Belief* out, I'm motivated and back on track. Instead of getting bogged down with details on who I will interview, what subjects I'll examine, and when and where I'll make those things happen, I decided I'd take the same approach I did with *Unlocking the Cage* where I let things flow naturally, doing things on the fly with no set plan, open to possibilities, one interview leading me to another. Through that approach I gained so many friends, heard so many stories I would have missed, and learned lessons I'd never know.

It also caused me a good amount of unnecessary head trauma because I couldn't say no to sparring and explain I was an out-of-shape 42-year-old with a history of concussions.

One of those concussions was sustained at Team Quest Gresham in Oregon when my head slammed off the mat and

TBI or CTE: What the Hell is Wrong with Me?

everything went black for a second. I finished that practice, had an awesome interview with Matt Lindland, then went back to the hotel with a pounding headache that stayed with me until the morning. Fortunately, I found a chiropractor who was able to relieve some of the pain and stiffness in my neck so I could go ahead with plans to visit Team Quest in Tualatin. I asked my buddy, Brian, to drive because I couldn't turn my head very far and the headache was still there.

At the gym, I left my training gear in the car, only bringing my audio and video equipment. Scott McQuary, the coach of popular UFC fighter Chael Sonnen, was teaching the children's class when we came in. I interviewed four of Scott's fighters before sitting down with him.

Scott, a life-long martial artist, touched on how it was the responsibility of coaches and managers to guide fighters and make sure they weren't too brave for their own good, one of my biggest faults as a fighter. He assured me that his gym had a family atmosphere and wasn't dog-eat-dog with animosity among fighters. If I wanted to give the MMA training a shot, I was more than welcome to join them.

Watching him coach, listening to the fighters he respected, and understanding how much he valued honor and integrity, I knew I could trust Scott. I told him about my neck issue and how it felt like I'd been in a car accident, but I left out that it'd been a concussion. He said not to worry and to go at my own pace, sit out if I needed.

The practice was very difficult and I wanted to quit several times, but I used the slogan on the back of Scott's Team Quest shirt to motivate me: Pain is merely weakness leaving the body. I finished the workout, and for the first time since I started the book project, I wasn't embarrassed joining the circle of fighters putting their hands together to wrap up the workout.

But now I've learned that one of the most dangerous aspects of a concussion is training before it has healed, I'm not nearly as proud of my decision to work through the pain, the motto of every sport I'd participated in since high school.

I'm thinking about the concussion because I'll be visiting Scott tomorrow. On my last trip he sent me a message asking if I'd be interested in hearing his concussion story. When I said I would, he made the same demand Michael Poorman had, insisting that his wife participate.

#

Scott's neighborhood in Lake Osewego is beautiful, everything green and clean. Scott, who's ten years older than me, greets me at the door and introduces me to his wife, Elisa, a charming woman who teaches for their school district. I get out my recorder and we sit at a table in their peaceful backyard.

In our first interview, Scott explained that he began training martial arts in fifth grade because he'd been getting bullied. Now that my focus is on head trauma, I ask him to recall his path and any concussions he might have sustained.

"I started with some boxing and wrestling," Scott says. "Gradually I evolved into the martial arts nerd with karate and judo and everything. With some of the throws, I might have lost consciousness a couple of times. I was hardcore judo for a long time and getting thrown three hundred to four hundred times per day. It's hard."

He says, "I did karate and kickboxing and stuff like that, but it wasn't until I got into my late teens, early twenties, that I really started getting into more of the sparring and other arts like the Dog Brothers. You think about their motto: Higher consciousness through harder contact. We wore the full Bell motorcycle helmets with our sticks, and it was not uncommon to see someone knocked out, and that's with a full helmet on. It was rough."

I share my times practicing Stickfighting and how it was brutal. A lot of pain and headaches in just the few times I'd picked up the sticks.

I ask, "When was your first major concussion or the first time you were scared by a blow to the head?"

"The first one was on my third and last MMA fight." Scott didn't start fighting until he was 40 and had managed to dominate the other sports he'd been in, such as wrestling and kickboxing, without taking any real damage. His first two MMA fights went well, and Scott got submissions in 30 seconds. But in the third, his opponent landed a clean shot to Scott's temple that knocked him out.

I ask how long he was out, but Scott says he doesn't remember it.

Elisa says, "He got hit like ten more times after he was out. They didn't stop the fight like they should have."

When the referee was asked why he didn't stop it, he told them, "Well, I always let title fights go longer. We always do."

Scott says, "I remember postfight talking to people. I felt okay. It wasn't until about three hours after the fight back at the hotel room that I got up to go to the bathroom and I got vertigo really bad and couldn't walk. She took me to the ER."

Elisa reminds him, "And you were throwing up for a while."

At the hospital they did a CAT scan and an MRI but simply said Scott had a severe concussion.

Elisa says, "The scary part is that it lasted a good ten to twelve months that he had symptoms of it. He had depression, loss of memory. It affected his vision."

Scott says, "I work in aerospace where I interpret X-rays of the jet engines, looking for flaws and I just was unable to concentrate."

The resulting poor work performance was making Scott's depression worse, so Elisa called his boss and explained that they had to treat the concussion as an injury and accommodate him. They did make the changes for Scott but let him know that if he continued fighting he would probably lose his job.

His symptoms worsened when he did anything that needed concentration. "As soon as I couldn't concentrate, I felt myself getting depressed, then I'd get frustrated and short-tempered. It was all the classic signs that I looked up of what a concussion entailed."

"Did you have any idea a concussion could last that long?"

"I didn't think it would. Like every fighter I thought it won't happen to me, I'll heal in a week. And then when it went on for months and months, it was very tough to get over."

Scott says, "That fight happened in 2006. In 2010 I was training jits and had someone in a submission hold. When I looked down, I couldn't feel them tapping." Fortunately for Scott, one of his students was a paramedic and realized Scott was having a stroke.

Scott recovered from the stroke and went right back to coaching. Two years later, Scott was getting Chael ready for the second Anderson Silva fight. They were doing an exhibition with Scott holding mitts for Chael, who wore bag gloves with no padding. Scott called out a spinning back kick, but the music was so loud that Chael heard spinning back fist. "He hit me clean on the side of the temple and dropped me. Four days later while training him and Yushin Okami, I ended up dropping in the middle of the training session. I had four grand mal seizures and bit through my tongue in three places. It was pretty traumatic."

Elisa says, "From the stroke he had similar things. He went into a depression again, forgetfulness. It took him a while even though he felt he was fine. As time went on, he would have lapses of memory and attention span that were obvious to me."

TBI or CTE: What the Hell is Wrong with Me?

I ask if there was increased anger or irritation.

"Absolutely," she says. "For the stroke there was more depression and some anger and frustration: but after the seizures I wasn't quite sure because they put him on a medication called Keppra, an antiseizure medication, and one of the side effects can be increased aggression."

It was obvious that would put a strain on any relationship. Elisa says, "You have to be responsible for your behavior within your relationship and family, but then you also need them to be forgiving and open." As a partner, Elisa says, "You've got to be deflective but accountable to whatever degree you can be and not just lay there and take it. There was definitely a lot of talking to be done trying to understand emotions."

They tell me that Scott's mood swings seemed to get worse later in the week, most likely after dealing with stressors of running the gym, dealing with work, and the family. Scott also suspects that it got worse at night. In the past when Scott would get edgy, Elisa would pack his gym bag and tell him to go work out, which meant sparring. Now that he was limited in what he could do physically because of the concussion, that only added to the depression.

Scott seems like an incredibly calm and peaceful person, so I ask how much anger or aggression he had before the events.

"I call it competitiveness. That's how I classify it," Scott says. "I've always been very competitive at everything and had a serene outer shell, but I like to compete."

When Scott was knocked out, the only medical advice they got was what they could find on the internet. After the seizure, they had a neurologist to consult with and new treatments to try.

One of the things Scott credits as being very helpful was playing brain games. "I also really got into a lot of meditation. I got into therapy and talked with the psychologist about how to alleviate stress, and it helped a lot.

"He does a lot of yoga and meditating, the Wim Hof breathing," Elisa says.

Referring to the different things that affect recovery, Scott says, "I'll be 58 this year. I question how much of the memory loss is from growing older and how much is from concussions. Sometimes I forget stuff and then wonder if I'm being too hard on myself."

I tell Scott and Elisa that my wife continues to insist that I'm fine, that I don't have any noticeable issues and I'm overthinking it. And then I completely lose my train of thought, which I laugh off as being due to the brain injuries.

The question comes back to me and I ask, "If you hadn't had any of the brain trauma, do you think you'd be much different mentally and emotionally?"

"I think the one thing it has done is it led me down the path of meditation, which was a blessing in disguise." Scott says he always had sympathy for his fighters who'd suffered brain injuries, but it wasn't until his own concussion that he had the empathy.

#

It's Saturday, the 90-minute drive to Astoria giving me plenty of time to replay the conversation I'd had with Michael and his wife and realize how similar their situation was to the McQuarys'.

Just as Scott could not have made it without the love and support of his wife, Michael had insisted the same, saying, "I would have crashed and burned my career without Sara. She gave up her career 15 years ago and my career became our career."

Sara said, "We had a normal functioning house with kids and dogs, but as the CTE progressed, we had to make the house predictable and quiet. He would sometimes need to eat by himself or leave." She turned their house into a non-target-rich environment, removing things that could be possible triggers.

She also explained the importance of creating a routine after the CTE. "It became necessary," she said. "He called a few times where he couldn't remember if he checked his luggage."

To make things easier for Michael, they planned his trip entirely, giving him cue cards, not only for business meetings, but for things like checking in at the airport. Sara said, "We can't change the world, but we gave him coping mechanisms so he could navigate it."

Even on family trips, they created a separate travel plan for Michael so he didn't become agitated from the added stress of taking care of them. All of this was an effort to protect her and the kids, and to protect Michael.

Sara said the goal had been to create an optimal environment for Michael literally losing his mind. "We had a whole retirement planned around his CTE. We were going to leave the country because we knew there wasn't good mental health care here. There's an island in the Caribbean that we really like. I'm an open water diver and I was going to start a dive shop and Michael likes to cook and so down there we'd done the calculations and we could afford to have a live-in caretaker. I envisioned having a little kitchen in the dive shop where he could cook. It's predictable, stable, low trigger, low pressure, something he could do every day."

When asked what else helps, Michael said, "I meditate. I say a series of mantras every morning. I read a lot of self-help books. I do cognitive therapy. Doing dishes or folding laundry is a form of meditation for me."

Michael said, "If I can be on a service-based orientation instead of a self-based orientation, and be aware of my emotion, I have a much better day."

I told Sara that my wife is convinced I don't have brain injuries. I asked her, "What would you tell my wife or the partner of someone who might have CTE?"

"First, you have to educate yourself on what CTE looks like. Understand the mechanics of it, the pathology and the progression of it. Then you need to understand the human aspect of what it looks like. YouTube is a great source for that."

Sara said that before the dissociative incident, she noticed peculiar things about Michael's behavior and questioned if it was just from getting old or angry. She also thought it could be marriage problems, wondering if she was at fault.

"It's not you," Sara said. "Educate yourself and get help through psychology or psychiatry. You can make adjustments to control it better. Get therapy for the whole family and teach children not to take it personally."

She said, "It's a Jeckyl and Hyde thing. Michael has done some hurtful and embarrassing things. It takes a really strong backbone to deal with it. I have emotional damage; my children have emotional damage."

Their 16-year-old daughter O'Shen confirmed just how difficult it had been. As a kid, she viewed her dad as a nice, caring, and genuine person who had random blowups, getting overly angry when it didn't make sense to be.

As a preteen, she couldn't understand why Michael acted like that and she internalized a ton of guilt. O'Shen thought she was doing something wrong and that she should be able to help. This contributed to four years of severe depression during which she hated herself.

Now that O'Shen's matured, she sees Michael as two different people. Through therapy and honest communication with both Sara and Michael, she overcame her depression and has a better handle on Michael's episodes. "It still bothers me, but I don't take it personally. You wouldn't yell at a paralyzed person for not getting up and walking."

O'Shen said it was sad, but one of the coping mechanisms is that she had to distance herself from Michael. "The rational side of me wants to argue with him when he freaks out, but I have to walk away and say sorry, just let it go."

When I asked her what she would tell someone else going through a similar situation, she said, "In the beginning stages, take advantage of the good sides that you get and the normal part of him you get, because eventually you don't get those sides as often."

Sara said, "I've seen the worst case things like Aaron Hernandez headlines, but it doesn't necessarily have to be that way. Michael has significant levels of CTE, but we're both motivated to keep our marriage and family together. We had to do unconventional things to deal with a peculiar disease."

By compartmentalizing the disease and behavior, their family has been able to have a high-functioning life with CTE. "If not, we would have divorced and he would have killed himself a long time ago," Sara said. "People are either going to be motivated to create a life around it or not."

Sara said, "I've come to terms with Michael killing himself impulsively any moment. I've locked up guns. At a certain point I said if he does it, he does it."

She related an incident that happened earlier in the week. A small thing set him off and he had a completely unwarranted response. "When something like that occurs, I make a calming motion to the kids. They'll put on headphones and leave. Sometimes calming things will bring Michael down or he'll go to another room and yell. It has to work itself out."

One thing Sara made very clear was that if you try to argue with someone with CTE it will escalate. "I could push Michael to suicide like that."

I asked Michael, "What would you tell other guys, guys you played football with?"

Although Michael hates the word surrender because it's the opposite of everything he'd been taught in athletics and about becoming a man, he said trust and surrender are the two biggest keys. "If Sara tells me that I'm having one of those episodes and moments, I have to trust her and leave, get out of that situation. Guys that are diagnosed now, I hope they are blessed with a partner like Sara."

He said, "We'll be having arguments where I know I'm right and then she plays the CTE card." Whether it's hand signals or knee squeezes under the table when Sara notices Michael's missing social cues or acting inappropriately, her drawing attention to the behavior is often enough to diffuse the situation.

Michael said, "I have a limited tank and I need to use all the resources in my tank just to make it through the day to be positive for my kids. The greatest impact you can have in your lifetime is how you can contribute to your family and community."

Taking a mood stabilizer was another suggestion they offered. Michael said, "We argued for six months before getting on Prozac. I didn't want to give up control."

Although Michael sometimes wonders if just the placebo would do the same, he thinks there has been an improvement. Sara agreed and said the Prozac slowed Michael down a bit to where he could see himself a little better.

Michael said, "The mindfulness has been a critical piece for me to gain control of my own emotions and to understand why I was insecure and try to let go of that. And by doing that it allowed me to trust Sara."

His advice to others was, "Practice mindfulness, meditation, mantras. Learn to connect to your emotions and understand your mental temperature. See a therapist and work on the underlying problem. And hopefully you're blessed with a partner that could educate themselves on it. Educate your family. It takes a team. Be humble enough to change your life according to the disease."

Chapter Seven

So my hormones are regulated and I'm in therapy, but despite the improvements, I am not in a good place. In fact, I'm pretty fucking angry, frustrated, scared, and regretful. Overall, just sad. And that doesn't include the guilt I have for feeling all this when I know what Michael Poorman and his family are going through, appreciating every moment they're together.

There has been some added stress thanks to the school year starting. Between taking my daughter and niece to school, along with my own doctor appointments, I'm spending two to four hours a day in the car. And if you've driven in Los Angeles, you're aware L.A. traffic stands for Largely Assholes.

But whatever the cause of the stress, I know the trigger. It's all this traumatic brain injury research. Reading articles and books is bad enough, but over the last few days, I made the mistake of watching videos of former boxers.

Michael Poorman pointed out in his interview that everyone knew boxing wrecked Mohammad Ali, so we knew the risk was there. But it's quite another thing to see the human side. These once powerful men, some of the deadliest in the world, were now in wheelchairs, barely able to speak and difficult to comprehend. Their families were in tears with no way to help. This wasn't some rare disease that only claimed a few random people.

The other thing Michael said about boxing was that he didn't believe he suffered any damage from the sport. Growing up, we were taught to get up and fire back. Fighting was a real part of life, blows to the head just something you shake off.

Back when I decided to fight, the thought of brain damage was not enough to dissuade me. Part of it was my complete disregard for my health and well-being, but the other part was that it seemed like a small risk. It wouldn't happen to me.

That's what I kept telling myself when I made the terrible mistake of attempting a professional boxing career with no prior boxing experience and just a handful of low-level MMA fights. When I moved to Vegas, I had an 0-1 pro record with very few rounds of real sparring. Things were about to get ugly.

I hadn't been in town long before someone thought it'd be a good idea to throw me against Friday "The 13th" Ahunanya, who was 15-0 with the majority of his wins by knockout. It took Friday half a round to figure me out. I walked into one of his right hands, bounced off the ropes and back into a second right that bruised my orbital and left me with double vision, slurred speech, and a headache for two weeks.

The next year I had one of my scariest concussions. I was sparring with my regular sparring partner, Kelvin "Concrete" Davis, who was a 17-0 cruiserweight at the time. It was the first round of sparring and I got shook with a hard hook. We paused so I could go to my corner to clear my head and get some water. Next thing I knew I was standing outside the ring with my manager, Wes, who was untying my gloves. I felt awful and apologized to him.

Wes asked what was wrong.

I said, "I couldn't even make it through one round of sparring." That hadn't happened since the bruised orbital sparring against Friday and I was pretty embarrassed.

But not as embarrassed as when Wes cocked his head and asked, "What're you talking about? You just finished four rounds and the last three were some of the best you've ever had."

Turns out that after the quick water break, I went right back to sparring for nine minutes, relying on autopilot because my brain was paused.

I played it off like I was okay, but in silence I was panicking. I didn't know what day it was and whether I had to go to my job at the prison where I worked graveyard shift. I also couldn't find my

TBI or CTE: What the Hell is Wrong with Me?

car keys anywhere, finally having to ask for help until realizing I'd been given a ride to the gym. It had slipped my mind that just a few days before, I'd totaled my car in a 70-mph collision with the center divider of the freeway. Obviously, my brain had not yet healed.

Over the next year, I continued to be brutalized by undefeated heavyweights and tough as nails journeymen that I'd watched fight on TV. All while partying like crazy, getting very little sleep, and eating only fast food and disgusting prison meals because I was living on a very restricted budget.

Man, that was not a good time for my brain, sabotaging myself at every turn. Fortunately, I got knocked out early in my fifth pro fight, and we all realized I was not cut out for the sport, my coaches and manager worried about my brain. Unfortunately, I didn't share their same concerns and went back into MMA.

Thinking back to the beatings was worrisome, but nothing like the phone call I just had with an old friend and sparring partner from the Golden Gloves gym. He had reached out years before when I was writing *Unlocking the Cage* as he was interested in doing a similar book for the boxing world. This time he called because he had questions about this brain book.

The conversation was one of the saddest I've ever had. His speech was slurred and difficult to understand, and he was an emotional wreck, his life in turmoil. At first he didn't think he had brain issues, but when I went over the laundry list of symptoms, revealing which ones were the worst for me, he admitted to each one. He had no idea any of what he was experiencing was due to head trauma. Head trauma that we had dealt out to each other.

Not long after the call, Jen walked into the kitchen and found me crying at the table, more videos of brain-damaged boxers playing on my computer. She tried to comfort me and asked what was wrong.

I said, "See all these guys right here? The ones that are fucked up and can barely keep it together before they kill themselves?"

She nodded.

Not trying to be melodramatic, just realistic, I said, "Yeah, well that's where I'm fairly certain I'm headed."

"No, you're not," she said, like it was a ridiculous notion. "You don't have those symptoms. Not more than the average person our age."

Because I only shared part of my emotional whirlwind with Jen, never wanting to scare her with certain admissions, she was partially correct in her belief. But when she walked away, here is what I wrote in my brain book journal: "If I do get dementia, don't forget to tell Jen, I fucking told you so."

I had three interviews set up to explore the military angle of brain injuries, but I blew them off at the last moment because the depression still had hold of me and I desperately wanted to distance myself from the subject. Jen insisted the research was negatively impacting our life and I should take a break or stop the book altogether. I was making my potential brain damage into something bigger than it actually was.

My sister, who also acts as my editor, was well aware of my brain research and suggested I check out Vital Head and Spinal Care in Pasadena where her son was having amazing results with neurofeedback and a specialized form of chiropractic that focuses on the upper cervical area. He'd been dealing with post-concussion syndrome for quite some time and seemed to have turned things around.

Just as I had with Millennium Neuro Regenerative Centers' protocol, I discussed the treatment plan with my wife, weighing the cost versus rewards. We both somehow still believed I was fine and didn't really need it but agreed I should at least see if the testing showed anything critical. If nothing else, it'd give me something to write about here.

TBI or CTE: What the Hell is Wrong with Me?

Still uncertain if I wanted to spend the money getting my brain mapped, I began with the NUCCA (National Upper Cervical Chiropractic Association) side of the practice. During my initial consultation with Dr. Julia Radwanski, she explained the difference between what they do and what traditional chiropractors do.

"What we look at is how the brain is communicating with the body," she said. "A traditional chiropractor looks at how the joints are moving, how the muscles are functioning."

Dr. Radwanski continued, "Your brain controls every aspect of your body. It controls all your muscles, all your sensations, your thoughts, emotions, organs, hormones, and so on. All that is passing through this tunnel here," she said as she pointed toward the base of the skull on her presentation chart. "If this shifts out of place, it causes inflammation and irritation here at the brain stem. When that happens, it changes the way that these signals pass through."

Knowing my history with head injuries, Dr. Radwanski said that with concussions the atlas, which is the topmost vertebra of the spinal column, can shift from left to right and also can twist from the top down.

My X-rays revealed a small, but significant shift of the two vertebrae (Atlas/C1 and Axis/C2) at the base of my skull. This was affecting blood flow and cerebrospinal fluid flow in, and out, of my brain. It was also causing my brain to get distorted messages from the sensors, called mechanoreceptors, in my muscles and joints, which was affecting my sense of balance and coordination.

Dr. Radwanski believed that shift was responsible for my ribs constantly slipping out of alignment, one of my legs being an inch off, the aggravation of the degenerated disc in my low back, and my twisted hips. She said, "You could work on these muscles all day, every day. You could see the best traditional chiropractor, you could see the best massage therapist, but if your brain is actually signaling for them to be tighter, they're going to stay tighter."

I committed to the practice, which meant driving to Pasadena twice a week for the first 8 weeks, but more importantly, giving up jiu jitsu and other activities while I'm in the healing phase. Part of me was excited there might be improvements, but the other part was annoyed to have another chunk of my day getting sucked up.

No longer having jiu jitsu to deal with aggression, frustrations, and worries, along with the added time in the car, is turning me into a terrible person to be around. Yesterday had started off well, but then I got into an argument with Jen. Instead of sticking around to finish the fight, I retreated downstairs, grabbed my computer, sat on the mats, and cranked up Slipknot as loud as it would go.

Jen appeared in the doorway and reengaged. My heart was racing, everything amplified, my emotions barely contained as I sat there. I turned down the music and attempted to talk, but she accused me of yelling and getting angry. The more she talked, the madder I got, feeling berated like a child as she stood over me.

I don't remember what she said, but questioning whether I had brain damage was a big part of it. I do remember that we were both yelling. She screamed something, and I lost it and leapt off the ground, landing right in front of her and shouting in her face.

Jen's scream pierced my brain.

I raised my hand like I might slap her. "There!" I shouted. "Think I don't have these symptoms? You want to fucking see them?"

Jen was stunned, silent for a second. Never in my life had I threatened a female. I was ashamed but still so angry. She kicked me out of the house, but I was already upstairs packing my shit, thinking of how I just completely screwed up my life, her life, the kids' lives, all in a matter of minutes, no idea how things had gotten so quickly out of hand. Never had I felt that loss of control. Never have I felt such shame.

TBI or CTE: What the Hell is Wrong with Me?

It's been a week since our fight. Although I've yet to forgive myself, Jen and I are doing much better. Before I had a chance to leave the house, Jen sat with me, and we talked everything over. She took some of the responsibility for pushing my buttons until I snapped and justified my anger flare by saying it was okay because I didn't hit her, even if it appeared I was tempted to. This attitude only made me dislike myself even more. I'd scared her so much that she was sounding like a battered spouse defending her attacker. I promised to Jen that if my behavior caused any of us to fear for our safety, I'd seclude myself somewhere safe or remove myself from the equation, a stance very similar to the one Michael Poorman had embraced.

I didn't tell my therapist that promise but did describe the whole fight. I was surprised he had the same understanding as Jen and told me I needed to forgive myself. Even though it doesn't seem that he gives the traumatic brain injuries much credit for any of my negative behavior, he understands my frustrations with my relationship and the continuing power struggle. He told me to focus on the positives that came out of the fight and taught me some coping techniques and how to approach Jen without causing another one. I also convinced Jen to do counseling with Harris's wife so both of us could benefit from therapy.

The NUCCA adjustments haven't made a noticeable difference yet, as Dr. Radwanski had warned, but I've been in a much better mood the past two weeks. And today was incredible, not getting stressed as I made the drive to California State University LA then to Pasadena to go over my brain mapping results with Dr. Giancarlo Licata, a NUCCA chiropractor and a very positive and energetic man who's always smiling.

Over the weekend, I had a great talk with my nephew, Ryan Nyeholt, who had benefited from both NUCCA and neurofeedback. Ryan's concussions from high school wrestling had been negatively affecting his life for the last year, headaches and the inability to focus causing his schoolwork and grades to suffer. After having his neck balanced with NUCCA and 30 rounds of neurofeedback, Ryan's grades had gone back up, headaches were gone, and he was a much happier and healthier person. The talk had been so convincing, that my wife and daughter also decided to have their brains mapped.

It was scary seeing what a concussion could do to a healthy young brain and the treatments it took to overcome it. I worried a bit about what my map might show, but I told myself all the hormone regulation I'd done had probably fixed any problems I might have had.

Dr. Licata began our conversation by mentioning the three windows that a health care professional looks at you through. One is the biochemical window, another is the mental health window, and the last is the physical window. If there is an imbalance in any of these areas, we should want to improve the major problems first and then the minors. If done in the wrong order, some treatments will not be as effective.

Fortunately, I already was addressing two of the areas. Dr. Alison Gordon had gotten my biochemistry where we wanted it, and the counseling, in combination with yoga, meditation, and the like, was helping with the mental health aspect. The NUCCA was addressing the hardware side of the physical window, and now the neurofeedback would be the software component.

It appeared my brain was primed for neurofeedback, but we still needed to determine if it would be the best modality to achieve my goals. My highest priority goal was to improve my executive function to get a better handle on emotional control and self-regulation. Next up was my attention and focus. Third, was my mood. Overall, I needed to react better to stress and develop a stronger impulse control. This included being able to stop using cannabis.

TBI or CTE: What the Hell is Wrong with Me?

Dr. Licata said neurofeedback should help me achieve all the goals, although it would take time. He pulled up the results from my Integrated Visual and Auditory (IVA-2) test, which measures the brain's ability to pay attention and to resist your impulses. (Image at back of book Testing and Scans)

The results were sobering. Despite my ability to test high on brain games and such, the IVA-2 had me pegged as ADHD and ADD, my auditory scores nearly half those of a normal man my age.

I've been competitive my entire life and have never been fond of being below average in any area, especially not when it comes to my brain. I never would have guessed that I could have ADD or ADHD symptoms, but the proof was right in front of me.

It was reassuring in a way to find out that even though I might be looking at someone and trying to follow the conversation, there was a good chance I wouldn't retain much of what was said. This explained a lot, and I was excited to tell my wife it wasn't due to me finding her boring or my not caring to remember. If I wanted to learn something, I would do much better visually.

But even scarier than the IVA-2 results was the prevalent dark blue of my frontal lobe qEEG (quantitative electroencephalography) images, which illustrated severely underfunctioning areas of my brain. This was not only compromising my executive functioning, but also was affecting my higher brain centers from regulating my lower emotional centers. In addition, we could also see how my brain was trying to adapt to chronic poor sleep, also probably caused by my past concussions. (Images at back of book Testing and Scans)

Improving my sleep is what Dr. Licata said had top priority. Sleep is really powerful, and we need both quantity and quality in order for the glymphatic system to get rid of the day's waste. Deep sleep is also responsible for releasing growth hormone, which helps new muscle start to form. And as Dr. Licata pointed out, I had been "chronically sleep-deprived for a very, very, very long time." By improving my sleep, many dormant abilities would be turned back on.

The second part Dr. Licata wanted to focus on is my executive functioning. By bringing the brain waves back to a normal range, I'd slowly regain control of my emotions. We would start with 40 sessions, first working on the foundation, slowly making connections, and then targeting different areas before reinforcing them. Ideally, I'd go for treatment three times a week.

Dr. Licata warned that the neurofeedback would almost obliterate my tolerance for cannabis. I was a little skeptical of the claim but said I was all for that. We talked a bit about cannabis and one of the dangers I had never considered. A recent study by the Amen Clinics showed that cannabis lowers blood flow to certain parts of the brain and those that use it regularly had overall decreased brain blood flow.[1] It was something worth looking into, but I doubted it would be enough to get me to stop using.

After seeing these results, the cost of the program wasn't a factor. If I could improve my diminished brain function, I was obligated to my family to try. When I got to my car, I gave Jen a call to tell her the news.

I had intended the call to be positive, to tell her the good news that I was going to improve my brain, but accepting I still had substantial brain damage had left me in a pretty dark place. Instead of telling her my frontal lobe was severely underfunctioning, I scared her by saying, "My frontal lobe is nearly gone." Not the same thing, but in my mind, it might as well be.

The drive home was depressing, a reminder there's a big difference between acceptance and peacefulness. I need to hope the

---

[1] Daniel G. Amen et al., "Discriminative Properties of Hippocampal Hypoperfusion in Marijuana Users Compared to Healthy Controls: Implications for Marijuana Administration in Alzheimer's Dementia," *Journal of Alzheimer's Disease* 56, no.1 (2017) 261-73

TBI or CTE: What the Hell is Wrong with Me?

neurofeedback will be enough to change my course toward self-destruction.

Chapter Eight

Thanksgiving is next week, a full four months since Michael Poorman's celebration of life. Even though his prognosis in March predicted he wouldn't be alive for the party, Michael was in great spirits, listening to friends and family share stories of him and telling some of his own.

It didn't take long to see what an impact Michael had had on so many lives. Friend after friend talked about what an incredible person Michael was, pointing out his loyalty and willingness to go out of his way to help. I began to worry a little though after the sixth person mentioned Michael was the kind of guy you'd call if you needed to hide a dead body.

I've been following Michael on Facebook, waiting for bad news but instead seeing prognoses extended. Instead of sitting around the house anticipating the end, Michael was travelling the country with his immune-filter mask on and knocking out an impressive bucket list, appreciating his family, and passing on the lessons he's learning from this experience.

I didn't expect to have another opportunity to say goodbye, but I'm about to board a plane to Phoenix so I can spend a few days with him and several other teammates from Brown that I haven't seen in 25 years. Michael knows he doesn't have long to live, and I'm honored he'd want to spend any of that precious time with us.

One of our teammates that made it to the Oregon gathering but isn't making this trip is Matte Zovich. The celebration was a very emotional event, and it was nice having Matte there to reconnect with. Matte's a gentle giant, one of the most genuinely nice people that I know. It was the first time my wife had met him and they hit it off immediately.

When I asked his impression of me at Brown, Matte's eyes widened and he asked if I was sure I wanted Jen to hear it.

TBI or CTE: What the Hell is Wrong with Me?

I said it was fine. Jen knew enough of my stories to realize how screwed up I'd been.

At Brown, Matte lived directly across the hall from me and had to put up with me blasting heavy metal all day long and seeing me either incoherently high or stumbling drunk, very seldom sober. He'd been the one I turned to when I smashed my mirror and had a huge shard of glass embedded between my knuckles. He helped clean up the blood and made sure I went to the student clinic to get stitches.

He also might have been the one who forced me to go back and get it reexamined the following week because my hand was swollen red to the wrist and hot to the touch. Not sure though. Like I said, most everything's a blur.

Matte reminded me of other things I'd blocked out of embarrassment, like using a razor blade to outline my tattoos before football games, the Rambo style knife kept on my nightstand, the 9mm tucked in the closet, riding my motorcycle without a helmet. Not exactly your average Ivy Leaguer.

While most of my friends went off to grad school or Wall Street, I was planning on becoming a cop or going into the military, something with excitement and risk. I was in a dark place with a death wish, longing for violence.

The talk with Matte helped me appreciate that I'd survived that destructive recklessness and managed to put a leash on the anger. When I got back home, I pulled out my box of memorabilia, searching for clues to my past, any signs of early violence.

It didn't take long before I came across three notebooks, one for each of the three years I attended preschool. My mother, in her impeccable penmanship, wrote down detailed notes as part of the program's requirement. Here's the summary:

At two years of age: Mark throws toys at siblings, is slow at speaking, loves puzzles, doesn't sing with others, no group activities.

At three years of age: Shy around other kids. Likes to tease and wrestle with older brother, plays cowboys and Indians, very affectionate. Insecure and withdrawn. Always fighting with brother.

At four years of age: Ornery. Won't stop behavior until forced to do so. Pouts if he doesn't get his way. Constantly fighting with siblings.

In grade school, I was a top student and stayed out of trouble except for a few fights. In junior high, I fooled most adults into thinking I was a good kid because of my grades and quiet disposition, but I was rebelling in all the wrong ways, becoming a vandal, liar, and thief.

In high school, my self-loathing escalated, and I began cutting myself, never enough to do any damage, but mostly for attention and a taste of pain. I began drinking heavily as a freshman and dove into cannabis the following year. Tired of hurting my hands punching holes in walls, I added a canvas punching bag to the weight room in my garage. After every training session, I'd finish up with at least ten minutes on the bag, refusing to wear gloves so I'd scrape my knuckles, bleeding all over the bag in hopes of one day completely covering it in brownish-red. Kind of sad that that was the extent of my ambitions.

The crazy days of college led to even crazier days afterward, throwing myself into MMA probably the only thing keeping me somewhat stable. But even while I did have this very aggressive side, I was the peacekeeper when it came to work. In all the years I worked as a bouncer and bodyguard, I never abused or took advantage of anyone, always trying to avoid or end fights peacefully. I was also an empathetic prison guard and probation officer, but that might have been due to my understanding that I easily could have been on the other side of the bars had I ever been arrested for my wrongdoings.

Games: Football's Concussion Crisis by Christopher Nowinski, Ph.D. I'd discovered the book when I was researching the Concussion Legacy Foundation (CLF). Chris is a cofounder and executive director of the nonprofit organization dedicated to solving the concussion crisis.

After writing the book in 2006, Chris cofounded the Sports Legacy Institute (SLI), which would change its name to the CLF. He also became one of the most influential voices in the push for concussion awareness and pivotal in getting the NFL to admit it had a very serious concussion problem.

Although Chris is a few years younger than me and a much better football player, we had a similar path. Our parents made us wait until high school to play football because they were worried about injuries. We both played defensive line in the Ivy League, me at Brown and Chris at Harvard, and we both graduated with degrees in sociology. While I went into MMA and boxing to further abuse my brain, Chris became a World Wrestling Entertainment (WWE) Superstar and suffered serious concussions, his post-concussion syndrome forcing him into an early retirement.

While learning about concussions to recover from his own, Chris realized that he'd had countless concussions playing football. Like me, and most players, Chris thought of them as simple dings or bellringers. Headaches, confusion, dizziness, double vision, ringing in your ears. That was all just stuff you dealt with. It was part of the game. Shake it off and get your ass back in there. No real man would take off a play because his head hurt.

Dr. Robert Cantu, who was at the time chief of neurosurgery at Emerson Hospital in Massachusetts, was the one who helped Chris understand what a concussion entailed. Instead of being defined as a physical injury, a concussion is a loss of brain function induced by trauma. The injury triggers chemical and metabolic changes, which together are termed a neurometabolic cascade of confusion.

Poor choices did lead me to two short stays in jail. Once in my twenties for driving while intoxicated and the second ten years ago for growing cannabis.

Desiring a better understanding of why I'd turned out to be such an angry young man, I delved into *The Anatomy of Violence* by Adrian Rayne. The book is fascinating, but it describes so many potential causes of violent behavior that I realized I'd never know what contributed to my disposition. Fortunately, the causes didn't really matter. All that mattered was what I did with the realization.

Everything I've been reading describes the correlation between traumatic brain injuries and cognitive and behavioral problems that could also result in aggressive behavior, violence, and a lack of insight and judgment. I don't want anyone to think I'm saying TBIs caused me to be a more violent person or that individuals with a TBI have the same problems as I do with aggression, anger, self-hatred, or impulsive decisions. But if I get across nothing else, it's that we must be honest with ourselves. How do I stack up against the symptoms?

Most people probably have a much different opinion of who I was because, like most, I kept the ugly side hidden. They don't know the suppressed thoughts and denied emotions. But Michael Poorman understood me perfectly.

After his party, we were joking about names for this book. Michael nailed it when he suggested *I'm More Fucked Up Than You Think I Am.*

#

The flight from LAX to Phoenix is only an hour, no time to get any real work done. I considered working on a short story that the trip had sparked about four former football players with brain damage who head out to the desert to go shooting, but I didn't need to freak myself out any more than I already was. Instead, I pulled out *Head*

TBI or CTE: What the Hell is Wrong with Me?

These changes in the brain create an increased need for energy as well as a deficiency in the ability to create the needed energy. This shuts the brain down to a certain degree and can cause a host of problems. The symptoms will range in length and severity depending on factors such as the individual's brain health, prior concussions, and the amount of time since the last concussion. Common symptoms include headache, dizziness, blurred vision, disorientation, confusion, disequilibrium, nausea, anterograde amnesia, neck pain, photophobia, sleepiness, fatigue, loss of consciousness, retrograde amnesia, and irritability.

Reading about concussions was scary, but all the stories Chris shared about high school and college football players having their lives ruined or lost in the days and weeks following concussions were maddening. The worst of these involved second impact syndrome (SIS), in which an individual suffers a concussion before the last one was resolved. Although SIS is rare, it is usually fatal.

SIS seems to affect teenagers more than adults, yet parents who are signing their kids up for contact sports like football generally have no idea this threat exists. As Chris points out in the book, much of the parents' lack of knowledge about the dangers was due to the NFL not taking responsibility for the damage they were doing, not only to their own players, but the kids they were encouraging to play. The NFL poured millions into youth programs while denying the danger of concussions; meanwhile, kids were killing themselves because their brains were scrambled.

The book is full of great points, but one that really stuck with me dealt with informed consent. We are now well aware that football and other contact sports can cause damage to an adult brain. A teenager's brain is even more vulnerable, and the damage is amplified for them, not lessened.

Children cannot provide informed consent before they are 18. They can't vote, drink alcohol, enter the military, or sign contracts.

So why can they participate in a sport that can permanently damage or cost them their life?

I had been stupid thinking there would be no consequences for my actions. I don't want to make the same mistake with my children.

#

Michael Poorman doesn't live far from the airport and told me I wouldn't need a car, so I pop my second cannabis gummy of the day and get an Uber.

My cannabis use has been lowered as Dr. Licata had predicted, and I had reached the point where I could take several days off at a time. I'm still consuming cannabis on a regular basis, just not nearly as much and usually beginning it later in the day.

Today's early use is due in part to being on vacation, but mostly due to nerves. Not knowing what to do or say around a person who is dying is a problem for a lot of people, and on top of that I'm anxious about reuniting with my teammates.

I remembered the names of the guys who will be joining us, but an awkward experience at a recent party at my friend Dan's house had me shook up. I was sober at the party, yet in three different incidents I introduced myself to people whom I'd known for years. Their nervous laughs and hurt feelings were still fresh in my mind.

Instead of meeting Michael at his house, he directs my Uber driver to an Indian restaurant where Michael and two of our friends are finishing up lunch. I'm glad to immediately recognize Tony Quarnaccio, who lives in Florida, and Jeff Moore from Virginia. They were both a year behind me at Brown and played defense; Tony at tackle and Jeff at safety.

TBI or CTE: What the Hell is Wrong with Me?

When I offer to shake hands with Michael, he asks me to first wash my hands. He doesn't go into details but says he's just gotten some bad news from the doctor and has to be extra vigilant.

After a nice time of catching up with everyone, we head to Michael's, where his wife, Sara, greets us and shows me the guest room I'll be sleeping in. When Michael excuses himself to change, Sara sits with the three of us outside to fill us in on Michael's situation.

Everything had been going surprisingly well with Michael's recent blood tests, but Sara received a troubling call this morning. Michael's numbers had dropped significantly, and if it were up to Sara or the doctor, Michael would be living in a bubble, his immune system too weak to fight off the smallest infection.

We all say we're happy keeping the reunion at their house or completely scrubbing it, but Sara shakes her head. "No," she says. "This is what Michael wants. If he dies while he's out with you guys, he'd die happy."

Sara goes over precautions we can take and things we should look out for. All of us are amazed at what a strong and loving partner she is.

A few hours later, the four of us drive to Top Golf to meet Alvin Huff, another friend from Brown. The old me would have refused to go with them because I'd never played golf in my life, but I'm happy to be here, not caring I'm the worst golfer. Over a couple rounds of drinks and golf, I listen to stories from Brown, none of them ringing a bell even though I had been present for most. Jeff even tells me about one where I was sitting on my bed, with my gun in my mouth. I remember doing that plenty but never with anyone around. It's a little troubling that all those memories have been wiped from my mind and all four of the other guys can recollect them, but it isn't worth worrying about.

By the time we make it back to Michael's house, we're both ready to turn in. We'll be leaving to go shooting in the morning.

Our good friend, Tom Hurst, shows up early with a truck full of guns to add to Michael's arsenal. Tom had also played defensive line and started at Brown when I did. He shares a photo I had completely forgotten about, shooting in the Arizona desert some 25 years before when I'd spent a few days with him while crossing the country on my motorcycle.

Alvin and I jump in Tom's truck, while Tony and Michael's son, Mateo, take another vehicle. We have a great time blasting through the ammunition, blowing away targets and clay pigeons, no one having a CTE moment and turning the gun on the rest of us as happens in the short story I'm working on.

Usually, I'd be jumping at the chance to shoot, but I enjoy sitting back and watching. It's a beautiful day and the weather is perfect. My favorite parts are when Michael coaches Mateo, the loving and strong support behind a boy who knows he is losing his father. It's painful to think this will probably be the last time they have this type of experience.

Back at Michael's house, I sit down with everyone while Michael helps out in the kitchen. Both Tom and Jeff have been paying attention to my brain trauma posts on Facebook and wondering about their own brain health. Alvin hasn't heard of it but is also a bit worried when I start explaining.

I dive into what concussions are, what they can do, and what symptoms might appear. The old me would be all doom and gloom, but I'm excited to tell them about the treatments. Without a doubt, neurofeedback, combined with the NUCCA therapy, and hormone regulation have completely turned me around. I bring up the results from my latest brain mapping and show them the giant leaps I've made, how my frontal lobe is now functioning much better. Now my IVA-2 scores are higher than normal and I no longer test for ADHD or ADD. And these results will only be improving as I've already started my second set of 40 sessions.

TBI or CTE: What the Hell is Wrong with Me?

The treatments have put me in a place where I no longer react as negatively to stress and I have much better control of my impulses. My friends are all interested but perhaps a bit fatalistic. Sara overhears some of the conversation and says that if they are at all worried about their brains, they owe it to their families to take care of them.

A bit later, we eat an amazing meal put together by Michael and Sara then go out to the hot tub. Michael can't jump in because of his health, but he's sitting right there beside Sara. I have to call it quits early because I made the mistake of taking a large dose of cannabis Michael had been saving for me. Sensing I'm not feeling great, Michael tells me to go lie on the bed while he brings Boris, their awesome emotional support dog, to me. I cuddle Boris and fall asleep, grateful for the friends I've reconnected with and for the lesson that Michael and his family have engrained in me: how to live your life with bravery, love, friendship, and positivity while facing death.

Chapter Nine

Michael Poorman passed away six weeks ago. He was surrounded with love: his wife, children, and Boris by his side. They played his favorite music and sang him to eternal sleep.

And here I am, happier and healthier than I've been in a very long time. I've got a lot of guilt over this, but Sara and Michael both made it clear how concerned they were for my future. They wanted me to heal within myself what I could and also share a message of hope and adaption.

Although I will never say that I've fixed my brain, I have most definitely recovered function. Even if I didn't have the brain maps and testing to back up my claims, I'd still know that things have changed for the better.

Eight months ago, I wrote the prologue to this book after experiencing severe depression largely brought on by attending a jiu jitsu event. Last night my wife and I went to watch our friends compete at Submissions on the Shore, unsure of how I'd react. Even though I was once again injured and unable to train, I was happy for my teammates who could. Instead of wanting to cry and hide from others, I was approaching people and telling stories. Despite the hour-long wait to get in, loud noise, and big crowd, the night was an exceptionally positive experience.

My outlook on life has improved drastically. The last entry in my daily brain journal was three months ago, an indicator that I've been feeling so good there's been nothing interesting to write about.

In addition to the positive mood, I've been incredibly productive and creative, already releasing *Untold Mayhem* and *Try Not to Die: In Brightside* with two more books scheduled to publish in the fall. I've achieved a nice balance between my family and my work, and I'm no longer getting as defensive and reacting as negatively to stress.

Opinions of oneself tend to be highly biased, and I've been known to exaggerate, so let's turn to the tests I took at Vital Head and Spinal Care. The following are the results from the IVA-2 test, which helps clinicians evaluate both visual and auditory attention and response control functioning. These tests were taken before the start of my neurofeedback sessions (August 6, 2019), after 20 sessions (October 29), and after an additional 20 (December 20). I retested on January 5, 2020, while sober and January 6 high on cannabis, but I'll save those results for another chapter. (Images at back of book Testing and Scans)

Improvements can be seen in all areas, but I like to look at the Sustained Visual and Auditory Attention Quotients, which measure a person's ability to respond to stimuli accurately, quickly, and reliably.

Before neurofeedback: Auditory – 77, Visual – 105

20 neurofeedback sessions: Auditory – 121, –Visual – 108

40 neurofeedback sessions: Auditory – 122, Visual – 112

My auditory score jumped 63% and surpassed my visual. It's also nice to see that I went from testing positive for both ADD and ADHD to now testing negative.

The qEEG images are a little harder to read, but I've included the most important ones at the back of the book along with other test results. The dark blue indicates severely underfunctioning areas. Light green are normal functioning areas. Red are overfunctioning areas.

My frontal lobe and left side of my brain were all dark blue and severely underfunctioning. Twenty sessions in, some of the darkness had faded to light blue. The second set of sessions dampened it even more, with a little bit of green sprouting.

I was thrilled with the improvements, but all that lingering light and dark blue convinced me to sign up for another 40 sessions.

I'll get retested and mapped next week when I hit the halfway mark, along with my wife and daughter, who are doing neurofeedback sessions, too.

It's also important to note that these improvements are from the combination of neurofeedback and the NUCCA treatments and that the gains would most likely not have been as great if I hadn't already regulated my hormones, been undergoing behavioral therapy, and doing all the brain activities on the side.

The improvement of my sleep, which was Dr. Licata's top priority, is probably the biggest reason why I'm feeling so much better. Although I didn't know it prior to testing at Vital, I'd been chronically sleep-deprived for a very long time, as indicated by my high delta waves. By lowering those waves and improving my sleep, I was also able to turn on many dormant abilities and raise the odds that I'd avoid dementia.

When I first started looking into brain damage, I read all the messages about the importance of sleep. The Concussion Legacy Foundation has sleep as the first item on their Living with CTE page. The Cleveland Clinic, supported by countless traumatic brain injury articles, agrees that one of the most important things you can do for your brain and overall health is get a full night's sleep. Lack of adequate sleep causes mental fogginess and headaches and affects self-regulation and emotion. Getting enough sleep leads to a healthier brain and can help rid the brain of the effects of CTE and other brain disorders.

I'd read those warnings when I believed I didn't have any issues and my brain was healthy. I'd gotten by with poor sleep most of my life and figured if I'd made it this far, there was no need to mess with it.

TBI or CTE: What the Hell is Wrong with Me?

My understanding of sleep changed last year when I read *Why We Sleep* by Matthew Walker, PhD. That book scared me and made me regret a lot of decisions, one of which I'm fairly certain is mentioned in the book.

It was my freshman year of college and I was at California State University Long Beach, broke as usual, selling the occasional dime bag of cannabis to help with gas money so I wouldn't have to ride my bike 25 miles each way. While browsing a bulletin board between classes, I saw an advertisement from the nearby VA hospital looking for volunteers to have their sleep measured. I can't remember how much money they were offering, but it was probably about $200, enough for me to volunteer.

Because it was so long ago, the details are fuzzy, but the researchers were measuring how lack of sleep would impact performance, mood, and memory, among other things. When it was time to fall asleep in the lab, they hooked up electrodes and an oxygen mask. The hardest part was having my arms strapped down. Throughout the night they cut off my air at different intervals during the night to rip me out of sleep, and they didn't want me pulling the mask off.

There was no window, so I could not see if there was anyone in the outer room; and despite knowing there were cameras on me, I couldn't help but worry someone might accidentally shut off my air and not realize I was suffocating. Once I overcame that fear I fell asleep, only to wake up gasping for air every time I was about to go into REM.

The extremely boring, repetitive tests I had to perform after waking in the morning were very irritating, and my mood declined quickly. By the third morning I became so irritable that I even called one of the workers a fat fuck, something I would never do in a normal state of mind.

After completing that study, the researchers mentioned another study they figured I'd be stupid enough to try. For this one, they sent me home with pills that would keep me awake during the weekend. I don't remember much about the experiment except that one night while hanging out at a friend's house in Hollywood I decided to go for a walk up and down Sunset Strip until sunrise because I was wired on the speedlike stimulant. The scariest part of this experiment is that I assume I was driving a vehicle while drugged and having zero sleep, an incredibly dangerous combination.

There may have been one or two other studies, but those memories are gone. I can't remember what my sleep was like prior to high school, but I'm guessing my parents made sure I got enough. Sophomore year is when things started going south, partying until two or three in the morning, not caring I'd have to wake up early for school or football practice. The late nights only increased through high school.

Things didn't improve during my first three years of college in California because I worked late nights as a bouncer, living on caffeine, often in the form of No-Doz. When I transferred to Brown, I immediately fell back into partying, often blacking out drunk and waking early to work at a nearby warehouse or to attend classes.

After graduating, I moved back to California where I worked as a bodyguard, often working graveyard so I could train MMA during the day and party on the weekends. There were way too many times when I nearly fell asleep at the wheel driving home from shifts.

A few years later, I moved to Vegas to pursue professional boxing, and my sleep grew even worse, working graveyard shifts at a prison and a juvenile probation facility. The lack of sleep caught up with me one morning while driving back from the prison when I had a single-car crash at 70 mph, totaling my car against the center divider of the freeway.

TBI or CTE: What the Hell is Wrong with Me?

Having my daughter and becoming a stay-at-home-dad in 2008 didn't slow me down. After a long day of taking care of Olivia while my wife worked, I'd crack open an energy drink at 9 o'clock to power through late-night writing sessions, only to wake four or five hours later to do it all again.

And if all that wasn't bad enough, of my last 11,000 nights of sleep, on at least 10,000 I went to bed stoned, many times with caffeine still flowing through my brain.

But still, I couldn't shake the engrained belief that I'd sleep when I was dead. My sleep was much better than that of many of my friends, and they all seemed fine.

Why We Sleep does an excellent job of pointing out why sleep is such a big deal. I won't go into any of the science as it can be extremely boring, but I encourage you to read the book and do your own research to verify anything you question.

Here are some of the main points in the book:

Losing out on any type of sleep, whether NREM or REM, will cause brain impairment.

Every major system, tissue, and organ in the body suffers with too little sleep.

All major diseases have causal links to lack of sleep.

The more you sleep, the longer you live. The less you sleep, the sooner you die.

It enhances our ability to make new memories and to learn new things.

Sleep makes us more attractive and reduces food cravings.

It improves our immune system and lowers our risk for heart attack, cancer, and diabetes.

Sleep is one of the most powerful performance enhancers and many professional athletes are paid bonuses for proper sleep as it boosts their playing ability and cuts down injuries.

A full night's sleep makes you happier, less depressed and less anxious.

Lack of it is linked to aggression, bullying, and behavioral problems.

Drowsy driving is just as dangerous as alcohol- and drug-impaired driving.

Lack of sleep increases addictive substance abuse.

Four hours of sleep will increase your chances of crashing nearly 12 times.

Sleep can help with healing most psychiatric disorders.

It is a key lifestyle factor for determining whether you will develop dementia.

As is the case with CTE, Alzheimer's is associated with the buildup of tau and beta amyloid. These and other harmful waste products are removed in the later stages of sleep, so a lack of sleep will only add to the accumulation of this toxic protein. This turns into a vicious cycle: the more buildup, the more impaired sleep becomes.

You do not know when you're sleep deprived.

All the above was enough for me to purchase a Garmin watch to track my sleep. I used it for a month or two, eventually giving it up because I hate wearing any type of jewelry or accessory and because I felt I was getting sufficient sleep.

But I began to take things more seriously when Dr. Licata pointed out that even though my quantity of sleep seemed fine, my brain wasn't getting the deep sleep it needed. I purchased a WHOOP wrist strap, which works like the Garmin watch, and had Vital monitor my results, adjusting my neurofeedback sessions accordingly.

According to WHOOP, I'm currently obtaining approximately 87% of the sleep I need. Although my sleep could be better, I'm content with the results. In addition to the NUCCA and neurofeedback, I was also following many of the suggestions

for better sleep that I found in Walker's book and online. These included the following:
- Giving myself ample time to get enough sleep and sticking to a schedule, sleeping and waking around the same time every day, even on weekends and during vacations.
- Making a to-do list for the following morning so I wouldn't worry about it at night.
- Improving my odds of quality sleep by creating a good sleep environment with comfortable bed and pillows and a cool temperature.
- Trying to exercise every day but avoiding anything too physical during the final hours before bed.
- Reading to help me relax and tire my mind.
- Cutting back on caffeine, enjoying it early in the day, and avoiding nicotine and alcohol.
- Napping during the day but no later than midafternoon.
- Getting rid of electronics before bed and using a blue-light filter.

# # #

Two weeks ago, COVID-19 was declared a pandemic. Last week, California issued stay-at-home orders. Today, I decided I'd better wrap up this book.

I'm trying not to get stressed over the situation and I keep focusing on the positives, like time spent with my kids that would have been wasted sitting in traffic. Social media and the news are full of fear and anger, so I've been steering clear of it and relying on my wife to figure how we should handle the situation. I trust her judgment and intelligence and am aware I'm likely to get sucked down a conspiracy hole or get frustrated with those that have.

With things getting a little scary, I'm keeping appointments to a minimum and switched over from brain training at Vital to a home version they monitor through Muse. When I went in last week for my monthly NUCCA checkup, Dr. Licata greeted me with a huge smile and a handful of papers.

He had my results from the Cambridge Brain Sciences tests I took prior to neurofeedback and again last week, some seven months and 80 neurofeedback sessions later. The test, which is used by healthcare practitioners and researchers to obtain accurate and quantified measures of cognition, was a fun challenge, but I hadn't paid any attention to my first set of results. Dr. Licata was very excited to show me those scores and compare them to the second set. (Images at back of book Testing and Scans)

I should point out that I took the first test in the late afternoon and the most recent test around 11 a.m. Perhaps that could account for some of the increase in scores, but I'm guessing not much.

The test measured 12 different areas, the increases and decreases in nine of those areas very small and balancing each other out. The other three areas showed significant improvements.

The Spatial Span, which measures the ability to remember information about objects in space and update memory based on changing circumstances, went up seven points, which took me from a ranking of the 67 percentile of men my age, up to 83.

An even bigger jump occurred in Rotations, which measures the ability to mentally rotate visual representations to reason about what objects are, where they are, and where they belong. This area increased by 15 points, taking me from a low 59% ranking to 90%.

The biggest jump occurred in the Spatial Planning task, which measures the ability to act with forethought and prepare a sequence of steps to reach a goal. This one jumped 32 points, pulling me from a 40% ranking to 97%.

Although it would have been nice to increase scores in all areas, Dr Licata had made it very clear from the start that we would only be working on certain areas of the brain at a time, most of the neurofeedback dedicated to improving sleep. If there were certain areas I wanted to boost, such as creativity or working memory, we would have to add those areas to later sessions.

In addition to the Cambridge results, we also went over my latest set of brain maps. Dark blue areas have faded into light blue and light blue has turned green. My brain is far from perfect or undamaged; without a doubt though, it is healing.

While all these positive changes have been occurring, I must admit I struggle with the worry that all of this is for nothing and that I'll still develop CTE and spiral into dementia.

When I brought up these concerns to Dr. Licata, he said we know enough about the mechanisms of the disease to feel confident it shouldn't develop. A big part of this is due to the improvement of deep sleep, which is of critical importance since this is where our body removes wastes like tau and beta amyloid that wreak havoc in neurodegenerative diseases like CTE and Alzheimer's. I was also treating overall inflammation with diet and supplements to avoid continually causing new damage.

Our talk made me feel a bit better and reminded me of one of the powerful videos on the CLF's website about the importance of hope. In the video, Dr. Robert Stern, director of Clinical Research at the Boston University CTE Center, stresses that CTE is not a death sentence and that you can treat symptoms. He states there's also a good chance that treatments will become available to slow down and possibly reverse CTE in the future.

I'm committed to adopting that mindset and believing that I have a bright future in front of me while understanding that we never know what might develop. All I do know is how much better I feel and that I'm striving in this time of stress instead of succumbing to it.

By treating the functional, emotional, and structural areas, I have attained a much healthier, happier, and safer place in my life. I believe I have significantly lowered the odds that I will develop CTE or another form of dementia. It has cost quite a bit of time and money, but it's a small price to pay when considering my overall health and happiness and the well-being of my family.

There are other treatments I want to explore and more experts to interview, but I am feeling much more hopeful now than I was at any other point of this process. And while I want to spread this message of awareness and hope, I'm also well aware that many individuals in my situation will not have the financial means to take advantage of some of these treatments.

Here is a rough estimate of what I have spent so far on my brain:

Millennium – hormone regulation – $3,000 for the year
NUCCA – $2,000
Neurofeedback – $9,000 for the mapping and 80 sessions
Therapy – $100 a session – $2,500 for one year
Supplements – $2,500 a year

This comes close to $20,000, a number that many cannot afford. But that doesn't mean that they can't heal and have hope. In these next chapters I'll take a look at the importance of all the things anyone can do for free and that have tremendous impacts on our symptoms and sanity. Our financial situation should not dictate whether we improve our life and brain health. Be committed to it, do the work, and improvements will come.

Chapter Ten

We're headed into the fifth month of the COVID-19 pandemic, and I'm not very hopeful it will end any time soon. I've still been staying away from the news and social media as much as possible, but my wife gives daily debriefings with updates on death counts, areas getting hit the hardest, and so on.

My thoughts on the pandemic are all over the place, but the best thing for my marriage and sanity is simply doing what Jen thinks is best. Although I wear a mask around others and we've been isolated as a family, I find it difficult not wanting to explore all the conspiracy theories. In *Ain't No Messiah* I had just written about the government killing off a significant portion of the population with a flu vaccine, and all the dystopian-type research I've done over the years makes it very hard for me to have faith in any government.

Aware of my tainted perspective and limited information, I've given up control like Michael Poorman did with his wife. I'll trust in my partner and will abide by whatever restrictions she thinks are best for my family and those around us.

Unlike so many others, we've been incredibly fortunate not to have our life turned upside down by the pandemic. After seeing the misery of friends losing family members and livelihood, I regret any complaining I've done during my life. There are always others who are truly suffering and in a much worse situation. This crisis just makes that more apparent.

Even with the added stress of having everyone home—meaning more cooking, cleaning, and video games—I'm still in a great place emotionally. I even began teaching writing classes with my kids on Facebook Live, something that I never could have imagined before. Providing this class, I don't feel like I'm doing much; but if we can help some other families find something positive and productive to do with their time, then I'm all for it.

On the writing front, I'm being very productive, and my coauthor, John Palisano, and I are putting the finishing touches on *Try Not to Die: In the Pandemic*. We worried that we were releasing the topic a little too soon and might appear insensitive, but John, who struggled with the virus and lost friends to it, helped me see that it's our job as writers to capture those things that feed our fears and frustrations. I've also managed to finish up *Beyond Brightside* and am excited to release both of the books around Halloween.

But even with all the household chores, playing with the kids, and writing, we're all going nuts being locked up. It was a nice surprise when my wife suggested we spend a few days at the beach for the Fourth of July.

The trip to the beach was a nice change of pace, a little bit of a break from the fear and loathing all around us. We did puzzles, played board games, went on walks, ran from waves, and got some reading in.

The book I disappeared into was *The End of Mental Illness* by Dr. Daniel Amen, a neuroscientist and psychiatrist. Although my mother has been praising Dr. Amen for years, this is the first book of his I've picked up. I had been planning to go to the Amen Clinic to undergo single-photon emission computed tomography (SPECT) imaging, which measures blood flow and brain activity, and then interview Dr. Amen for this book, but the pandemic has convinced me to sideline that plan.

I have mixed feelings about not following through with the Amen Clinic. Having another scan could increase my confidence that my brain is in a state of healing, but there's also the risk of discovering more things wrong with my brain. And although I wanted to talk with Dr. Amen about the effects of cannabis on the

TBI or CTE: What the Hell is Wrong with Me?

brain, I know I won't like his answers. The testing would also come with another price tag that I can't justify. His book will have to do. I often dread picking up nonfiction books, afraid they'll bore me to death, but I was pleasantly surprised by Dr. Amen's book, which is easy to read and understand. The book explains how neuroscience can help prevent or reverse many disorders and brain issues that have been classified as problems with mental health, a term Dr. Amen argues should be thrown out and replaced with brain health. With most physical complaints, doctors will order some sort of scan, such as X-ray or MRI, to determine what the problem is, but for far too long, psychiatrists have diagnosed mental health problems simply based on behaviors and reported symptoms, with no real idea of what is going on in the brain.

If our brain is healthy, then our mind is healthy. Problems arise when the brain is unhealthy. People are not mentally ill, it's their brain that is unwell. This change in terminology would likely lower the stigma, guilt, and shame that are associated with the illness, and encourage more people to seek help.

Dr. Amen's clinics have performed more than 170,000 scans on patients, giving him an incredible wealth of data. Through the use of SPECT imaging, he can see which portions of the brain are over- or underfunctioning and create treatment protocols based on science and not a loose-fitting diagnosis like PTSD or ADHD. SPECT images found throughout the book paint a very clear picture of what dysfunctional brains look like after strokes, Alzheimer's, brain trauma, drug and alcohol abuse, and other harmful conditions.

Early on in the book, Dr. Amen describes common SPECT patterns that guide diagnosis and treatment. He also lists the 11 brain health risk factors, making them easier to remember with his acronym BRIGHT MINDS.

Blood Flow

Retirement/Aging

Inflammation
Genetics
Head Trauma
Toxins
Medications
Immunity/Infections
Neurohormone Issues
Diabesity
Sleep

    Although my brain has been negatively impacted by multiple sources, the one I'm most concerned with here is head trauma. The brain is radically changed by a TBI, which makes sense when we look at from the effects of the trauma. These include bruising, broken blood vessels and bleeding, increased pressure, lack of oxygen, damage to nerve cell connections, tearing of brain cells which spill proteins that cause inflammation, and major hormonal imbalances if the pituitary gland is affected.

    The brain rehab program Dr. Amen recommends for TBI consists of neurofeedback, hyperbaric oxygen treatment (HBOT), supplementing with nutraceuticals that have health-giving additives and medicinal benefits, engaging in brain-healthy habits and avoiding unhealthy ones. I had planned to try HBOT, which provides people with concentrated oxygen in a special pressurized chamber, but as with the SPECT scan, I'm going to concentrate on the other things I can be doing.

    I recommend that anyone who wants to better understand the brain and how to improve, it pick up *The End of Mental Illness*. It's a quick read packed with easy-to-process information. I finished the book in the two days at the beach, and it, along with my narcissism, has convinced me to finally get back into regular exercise and healthy eating. I was embarrassed having my shirt off at the beach and disappointed in how much I'd let myself go. Knowing I need to be held accountable to reach my goals, I posted on social media that I would reach 205 pounds by my birthday in August. Dropping 23 pounds in six weeks won't be easy, but I'm determined.

# # #

It's been two weeks, and I've already dropped 12 pounds with 11 more to go in the next 30 days. In addition to the radical changes to my diet, I've finally fallen back into a good exercise routine and feel better than I have in quite some time. Thanks to the bets I took at the start of this, I'm incredibly motivated to achieve my goal. If I fail, I give up cannabis for one month, something I'm not prepared to do during the pandemic.

For something I've loved most of my life, it's surprising how easy it is to fall away from exercise. As a child, I was always in the backyard chasing my siblings, climbing trees, and digging holes. Every recess and lunch break at school was spent playing football, soccer, or some other type of sport. I was introduced to weightlifting in seventh grade and it quickly turned into an obsession. I couldn't control that I was on the small side, but I believed that with hard work and dedication I could become stronger, faster, and tougher.

In high school and college, powerlifting and kickboxing filled my days, at least when I wasn't playing football. After graduating, I transitioned to MMA and boxing, training religiously to improve my chances of not getting my ass kicked too badly. It wasn't until I tore my Achilles tendon in 2005 that my relationship with exercise hit a decline.

At least once a year, I'd make an attempt to get back into shape, jumping on the latest fad and picking up a piece of equipment only to use it for a month or two and giving it away the following year to make room for the next piece that would hopefully reignite my passion. Nothing seemed to stick, and I put on more and more weight as my body grew weaker. Finally, I had enough and began *Unlocking the Cage*, forcing myself back into shape with MMA training. After two years of taking blows to the head, I made the switch to jiu jitsu and yoga and became healthier than I had been in a long time.

Soon after I started my research into TBI, I told Dr. Alison Gordon that I was worried that my decline in overall mood might have been tied to my brain injuries. She helped me understand that it was much more likely due to my lack of exercise. Shoulder and neck injuries had kept me off the mat and out of the yoga studio for quite some time, and I was miserable. Her reminder was enough for me to seek out help and fix the problems that were holding me back. A few cortisol shots, stem cell injections, and a ton of physical therapy enabled me once again to return to the activities I enjoyed.

Just as for sleep, every TBI article I've read lists exercise as one of the most important things we can do for our brain health. The Concussion Legacy Foundation's Living with CTE page states: "Regular exercise can relieve stress, help with pain, and improve overall well-being. And remember, what is good for your heart is also good for the vascular system in your brain."

And also, like sleep, exercise impacts every system in the human body, and everyone benefits from it. It helps us control our weight, combats unhealthy conditions and diseases, improves mood, boosts energy, gives you better sleep, and can make sex better. Recommendations vary on how much exercise is needed, but recommendations range from 75 to 150 minutes of aerobic activity a week, or roughly 20 minutes a day, along with at least two days of strength training.

Dr. Amen's book gives a great breakdown of how exercise helps our brain health. He states that 100 minutes of exercise a week, along with a healthy diet, decreased brain age by a decade. In addition to everything mentioned above, he points out that regular exercise lowers the risk of developing depression; increases the size of the hippocampus while protecting it from stress-related hormones; stimulates brain-derived neurotrophic factor (BDNF), which improves plasticity of the brain; stimulates the ability to generate new neurons; improves cognitive flexibility; increases oxygen and nutrient delivery; and allows for greater detoxification.

The four types of exercise he recommends for brain health are—

- Burst training involves short bursts of exercise near your maximum heart rate followed by lower-intensity exercise or rest between bouts. This could be any kind of exercise, such as running in place, jumping jacks, squats, jump rope, biking, and swimming. The benefits are a raise in endorphins, improved mood, and more energy.
- Strength training also increases mood and energy while reducing anxiety. This does not just mean lifting weights. It also includes using resistance bands and doing bodyweight exercises.
- Coordination exercises boost activity in the cerebellum. These could include table tennis, dancing, juggling, and ball tosses.
- Mindfulness exercises help increase focus and energy while lowering depression and anxiety. These include yoga, Pilates, and tai chi. However, nearly any exercise or activity can be turned into a mindfulness practice by focusing on your breathing and being present.

The whole COVID-19 situation has made exercise both easier and harder to stick with. While options like going to the gym to do cardio and strength training are gone, I have enough equipment at home to get as good a workout. The same goes for being able to practice yoga and jiu jitsu at home with my wife and kids, since most studios are closed.

I have more time in the day to exercise thanks to the pandemic, but it has also done a number on my motivation. When you're laid back and comfortable, getting up to exercise doesn't sound like fun. Sitting on the couch and playing video games is much easier to settle on than going for a jog.

But what I'm discovering again is that the more I do something, the easier it is. Additionally, the more variations of exercise I include, the greater the chances I won't get bored and abandon the activity.

In the last decade, yoga and jiu jitsu have been my favorite ways of staying in shape. Jiu jitsu feeds my competitive side, improves mental and physical toughness, and works my brain as I learn new and challenging moves. Not to mention just how much I enjoy the social interaction, rolling with people you might never talk to on the street, everyone equal on the mat, financial, educational, and relationship status not meaning a thing.

Since I began the weight loss challenge, I've been doing a lot of rowing on my Hydrow machine. This has been great for my body and feeds a bit of my competitiveness but rowing indoors is still relatively boring.

Doing small bursts of activity throughout the day has been effective, especially helping me with creativity and overall mood. Every day is different, but I find doing a few sets of push-ups, crunches, and squats during the day gives me the peace of mind from knowing that at least I did something physical.

The most powerful form of exercise for me is something the old me would have slapped me for saying 20 years ago. Yoga. It is awesome, plain and simple.

Like many males, I always looked down on yoga and thought it was for women. But then I trained jiu jitsu with Anthony Johnson, a former Marine. For a big, strong, and technical jiu jitsu player, I couldn't believe how well Anthony moved, the control he had over his body, and how immense his gas tank was. He attributed all that to his yoga practice, and he said if it hadn't been for yoga, he wouldn't be able to do anything at all thanks to a degenerated disc in his lower back.

Shortly after I met Anthony, I tore a ligament in my knee and was looking into getting surgery for it. He convinced me to let him help me rehab it with yoga. I thought it was impossible but gave it a shot, discovering that I was able not only to recover function in that knee, but also to improve it quite a bit while strengthening my entire body.

What matters now is that I've been doing something daily. Sometimes it's not much, but even the littlest things make a difference in my mood and energy. I am not only helping myself become healthier, but also being a better role model for my family and showing them how to work toward goals.

The most important thing to remember is that there's no one right exercise for everyone. Experiment with different forms and find the ones that work best for you to improve your odds of sticking with it. If you've been sedentary for some time and don't know where to start, I recommend aiming for a 15-minute walk every day.

#

I was proud that I hit my goal of 205 on August 19, my 48th birthday. I'm even happier about weighing in this morning, seven weeks later, at 199.6, the lowest weight I've seen since I was 16.

Although exercise over the last four months has played a part in losing the weight and improving my mental well-being, I wouldn't have had a quarter of those results if I hadn't transformed my diet.

I generally try to eat healthy and cook organic food, but as the pandemic dragged on, we'd been ordering food more than usual. I knew I had to change that and late-night snacking if I wanted good results. Fortunately, I had my good friend, Fortunato Lipari, put together a meal plan that focused on a keto diet and intermittent fasting (IF).

For those not familiar with it, a ketogenic diet is a high-fat, adequate-protein, low-carbohydrate diet that forces the body to burn fats rather than carbohydrates.

The intermittent fasting is what it sounds like: not eating any food for specific amounts of time. This type of fasting can significantly improve mood, memory, weight, blood pressure, memory, and inflammation. Fasting 12 to 16 hours turns on the autophagy process in which our brain gets rid of the waste it accumulates, just as it does during deep sleep.

I had tried IF a few times before but never made it past a week. Fortunato understood this and started me off easy, stressing the importance of what we cut out, mainly unhealthy carbs and sugars.

The first items to go were the energy drinks and teas I'd been consuming. The teas had 130 calories, mainly from added sugar. Most of the energy drinks had zero calories, but they were full of preservatives and ingredients I didn't need. In addition, cutting the ridiculous amount of caffeine helped ease my fear that one of these days I would have a heart attack or stroke.

To help my commitment to cutting them out, I took all the money I would have spent on the drinks and stuck it in a jar. Yesterday my son and I counted the money and donated a little over $300 to a neighbor who'd been struggling due to the pandemic.

As for the fasting, I began with 12- to 14-hour fasts and eating two meals a day. Every week, I would extend the fast for an hour or two until I was constantly hitting 18- to 20-hour fasts, often only eating one meal a day. I even added in some 36-hour fasts and went as far as 40 hours once.

I may have been too extreme with the fasting times and most likely lost some muscle mass by rushing things, but I can't stress how much better I felt physically and emotionally. The majority of this heightened sense of well-being was probably due to the severe reduction of sugar intake.

The change in eating revealed to me just how little food I need, how much I'd been overeating, what an unhealthy relationship I'd had with food, and how addicted I was to stuffing my face. During fasts I would find myself in front of the cupboard only to realize that I wasn't hungry at all, just bored or looking for a way to find calm. I also realized that I was viewing food as a reward, not as a source of fuel and nourishment.

Most of us understand that the amount and type of food we consume have a huge impact on our body. It can lead to our becoming overweight, undernourished, and at risk for the development of diseases and conditions, with arthritis, diabetes, and heart disease being three of the big ones. But not many people consider how what we eat affects our brain. In *The End of Mental Illness* Dr. Amen lists many of the dangers we should avoid. Here are some of his recommendations:

- Eat organic food and always wash produce to reduce the amount of pesticides consumed.
- Read food labels and avoid chemicals, additives, and preservatives like MSG, Red Dye #40, and artificial sweeteners.
- Avoid fried food and processed meats while sticking to high-quality protein, like fish, chicken, beef, turkey, pork, nuts, beans, and legumes.
- Don't use vegetable oil and eat and cook with high-quality fats, like avocados, coconut, nuts, olives, seeds, and seafood.
- Drink plenty of purified water, limit alcohol, and avoid energy drinks and sodas.
- Eat complex carbs high in fiber, like vegetables and certain fruits, while avoiding cookies, candies, bread, and pasta, which cause blood sugars to spike, then crash. Sugar adds to inflammation, increases diabetes, and promotes aging. High-sugar

diets and blood sugar problems are associated with schizophrenia, irritability, anger, trouble concentrating, anxiety, depression, and addiction to sugar.

- Eat plenty of foods that are rich in antioxidants as well as herbs and spices, like turmeric, rosemary, cinnamon, peppermint, garlic, and ginger.

Dr. Amen also goes into detail on supplements you can take to aid your brain health, but there are too many to list here. Please remember, I'm the furthest thing from a doctor, health care provider, or the like. Do your research and talk with a functional medicine doctor or other knowledgeable person before beginning any radical diet or taking supplements you're not sure of.

Most importantly, treat food as a fuel and do as Dr. Amen says: only eat the foods that love you back. Your body and brain will thank you.

Chapter Eleven

The riot at the Capitol took place two weeks ago and this country is divided like never before. It seems as if everyone has nothing but hate and contempt for those with the opposing viewpoint, but I block out all the negativity and focus on controlling my reactions to the outside world. And right now, all I'm feeling is pure joy because I just heard the results of my mom's last set of brain maps from Vital Head and Spinal Care.

Dr. Licata hadn't shared much about her first test results because he was afraid it would cause her more anxiety. My mom, who is 77, had chronic poor sleep and a sister with advanced dementia, and her brain's processing speed was significantly slow compared to other women her age, an indicator she could be considered predementia/pre-Alzheimer's.

After 40 neurofeedback sessions, my mom's sleep improved in both quantity and quality. The dark blue areas of her brain map faded to light blue, and her processing speed improved so significantly that she is no longer considered predementia. Because there was still room for improvement, we scheduled 20 more neurofeedback sessions and asked what else we should be doing.

Dr. Licata shared that people who don't have jobs that require new learning will develop memory and brain health problems, and retirement, which is often a state with little new learning, only adds to this decline. The brain needs to be exercised just like a muscle, and by hitting it with different approaches, it will create new connections while maintaining and improving other areas.

Fortunately, my mom was aware of this and was pursuing learning new things with friends in a group created by a woman helping her mother with Alzheimer's. In addition to sharing information about ways to improve their minds, like breathing correctly and practicing different types of exercise, they also benefited from interacting socially and meditating. For the new learning, the women played a variety of different card games to work on concentration and memory, along with I Spy, marbles, badminton, and billiards.

While this group is a great idea and I'm glad my mom is part of it, they only meet once a week. One day out of seven isn't sufficient. If it were up to me, I'd prescribe doing ten minutes of an activity for each of the brain regions every day.

There is an excellent image in *The End of Mental Illness* called Brain Health Workouts by Region that shows which types of activities help different parts of the brain.

- The prefrontal cortex, which was the biggest problem for me, can be worked on with language games such as Scrabble, crossword puzzles, and strategy games such as chess.
- The temporal lobe is worked out with memory games and memorizing poetry and prose.
- The parietal lobe can be exercised with activities such as math, juggling, map reading, and golf.
- The basal ganglia is hit with balancing, manipulating props such as ropes and balls, and synchronizing arm and leg movements.
- The cerebellum is worked out with coordination games and activities such as dancing, basketball, tai chi, yoga, and table tennis.

When I began worrying about my brain, I added new learning as a precaution, beginning with Lumosity. I work different parts of the brain by varying the games using speed, memory, attention, flexibility, problem solving, language, and math. I used to play the games more but now generally try to fit in five to ten minutes a day.

One of the best things I added to my routine is playing music. Playing an instrument is a full-body workout for the brain, recruiting regions that process vision, sound, movement, and memory. Studies have shown this can result in long-lasting

TBI or CTE: What the Hell is Wrong with Me?

improvements in structural and functional brain changes and may enhance neurogenesis, which is linked to improved learning and memory activity.

Although listening to music has been an important part of my life since I discovered Iron Maiden at ten, I never felt I had any musical ability. Doubting I could learn, I started off slowly, picking up an electric guitar to play on Rocksmith, a video game on Xbox. Although I didn't gain much from the game, it increased my desire to learn. For Christmas, my wife surprised me with an acoustic guitar, and I began using the Yousician app to teach myself how to play. My first year on the app I practiced a little over 100 hours, which was roughly the same amount of time I spent watching television.

Because I enjoyed playing so much, I've since picked up a bass and another electric guitar and now switch between the three instruments for even more of a challenge. The goal is to play for 20 minutes a day, and while that doesn't always happen, there are many days when I'll play much longer.

I'm sure it would be much less painful to listen to me play if I had ever taken real classes or private lessons, but I've gotten rid of my perfectionist habits and am happy to simply practice. The solitary time with the app has been great, and whenever I want to make it more fun, I'll beg one of my kids to pick up an instrument and join me. By not worrying about being an expert and simply enjoying the moment, I now look forward to playing guitar and probably will for a very long time.

In addition to the music, I decided to learn a new language after reading that it was one of the most effective and practical ways to increase intelligence and keep the mind sharp. Language learning helps improve thinking skills and memory and can develop new areas of the mind. It can also strengthen the brain's executive function and natural ability to focus, something I desperately needed before I rehabbed my brain with the hormone regulation and neurofeedback.

Looking for a challenge, interested in my German ancestry, and being a huge fan of the band Rammstein, led me to study German. I spent a lot of time trying out different apps such as Rosetta Stone and Memrise. My longest streak was on Duolingo at 324 days.

Despite all the time I've spent learning German, I haven't taken advantage of tutors or put in enough practice to become fluent. I'm good with that though, just as I am with the guitar. I'm learning a little bit every day and working my brain. As long as I put in the effort, I'll gain the benefits.

The last few years I've been listening to an outrageous amount of disturbing German heavy metal, usually with headphones for my family's sake. I'm discovering this is an interesting and fairly passive way for me to work my brain, expanding my vocabulary and improving pronunciation. And even though I don't feel that I can yet have a decent conversation with a native speaker, I can read a fair amount and I'm looking forward to visiting Germany to do readings from my German-translated fiction as well as this book.

There are so many languages to choose from, different musical instruments to pick up, and types of games and activities to play. I can't think of a good reason not to begin at least one new form of learning. Even the busiest person can find time to fit in ten to fifteen minutes a day, whether it be while driving, taking a bathroom break, or before sitting down in front of the TV. Experiment with different approaches until you find the right ones for you. Find a couple that bring you enjoyment and see how much they improve your well-being.

#

This next suggestion for brain health and dealing with TBI symptoms is one of my favorites. Writing, an ability I used to associate with nerdiness, is one of the most consistent things that I've been doing for my brain health even though I didn't realize how it was benefitting me.

The first suggestion on the Concussion Legacy Foundation's Living with TBI page is to write things down to help with productivity and gain a sense of control. I never liked the idea of creating a list, but for the last four years I've been living by them. Both my short- and long-term memory are terrible so the list helps me remember appointments and lowers my anxiety that I might forget to do something having to do with work or family. Checking off completed items the next day adds to a sense of accomplishment, and those tasks that don't get finished are simply moved over to the following day.

The second suggestion on the CLF's Living with TBI page is to develop a routine to create a sense of stability and make life more manageable. Michael and Sara Poorman helped me understand how crucial this was for them. Everything was scheduled and written down. Michael took notecards with him everywhere, whether to a board meeting or on a business trip, giving him confidence that if he had trouble thinking, his tasks or talking points would be right there for him to access.

Keeping a journal or diary is another powerful tool at our disposal. Before writing this book, the only journals I wrote in were weightlifting and martial art diaries in which I would keep track of weights and techniques. At the start of this research, I began a brain journal in which I write down anything significant that happened during the day. Some days it would be a few sentences, other days a couple of paragraphs filled with negative reactions to stress, verbal escalations, road raging, how much cannabis and caffeine I'd ingested, whether I'd meditated, and so on.

Without the journal, I wouldn't have been able to look back and honestly say how I'd been feeling or what I was thinking. This journal has been crucial for writing this book as I can go back and use my exact words about an experience. It also helped me deal with the emotions while writing down and examining them at the time, holding myself accountable for undesirable behavior and acknowledging moments I was pleased with. And with the journal, I did not have to hold anything back worried that I would be judged. This approach would be great for someone who's too embarrassed to confide in a therapist.

Keeping a gratitude journal isn't something I'd ever done until a few weeks ago. There wasn't a huge benefit to the journal, but I realized that was only because I'd already made it a nightly routine to practice gratitude when I would use cannabis. Expressing gratitude to ourselves and others induces positive emotions and impacts our overall health and well-being by lowering fear, anxiety, and depression while also improving sleep.

My least favorite form of writing is what I'm doing right now. Writing nonfiction, examining myself and my fears, putting my life out there and being vulnerable. Nonfiction takes me away from my fiction and is much harder for me to stay focused on. I find it tedious and too scholarly and would much rather spend that time thinking of cool ways to kill off characters.

But I understand how beneficial writing nonfiction can be. As with the brain journal, writing about oneself and personal experiences can improve mood disorders, reduce doctor visits, and even boost memory. The finished product can also help those that read it because they no longer feel as alone and are exposed to a different perspective.

Writing fiction has been my passion for the last 25 years, and the urge to write never goes away. I have well over 15 years of work already scheduled and am fairly certain I'll write until my brain fails me. Maybe all my writing won't be dark and disturbing,

TBI or CTE: What the Hell is Wrong with Me?

but I wouldn't bet against that. Being able to create entire worlds and casts of characters is a blast, and I get an extra kick out of doing that with coauthors for my *Try Not to Die* series.

I never gave much thought to why I wanted to write or what I was getting out of it, but there's no denying the act is an incredible catharsis. Whatever I'm dealing with at the time is what comes out in my work. The overall theme of my writing deals with my fear of death, but I delve deeper into the human condition in each book. *Brightside* was about suicide and having dark thoughts. *25 Perfect Days* was my disgust with the world and atrocities both religions and governments have committed. *Aint No Messiah* was similar in nature with a healthy dose of dirty sex on the side.

In more than 100 short stories, I've hit a myriad of facets of my life that needed release. A failed marriage. A shitty fighter. An unknown author. A thief and a liar. A disappointing son. A forgotten father. A reckless teenager. A backstabbing friend. A drug addict. An alcoholic. A man with a wrecked brain.

In fiction, we can dive into imaginary characters and flesh them out, deciding how their background and experiences have shaped them. Through these characters we can safely explore our fears, frustrations, and weaknesses. We can express love, gratitude, or any other positive emotion. We're free to write whatever we want, something I find similar to the brain purging its waste at night. I get all the dark, ugly stuff out of me so it doesn't accumulate.

Although it's difficult to quantify how much writing has helped me, I love pointing to the experience my friend Anthony Johnson had from working on our book *Try Not to Die: In Iraq*. Anthony, an Iraq war vet, struggled with debilitating night terrors after he got out of the military, but after working on our book for a month, Anthony's night terrors were greatly reduced. Whether it was due to our talking about what he'd experienced or him fictionalizing the events, his well-being improved significantly.

I consider directed writing the most powerful form of writing. I discovered this when I attended Tom Spanbauer's Dangerous Writing retreat in 2008. The focus of the retreat was to create a short story based on a moment that changed who you were as a person. I went into the weeklong course feeling as if I didn't have anything important to write about, but while there I had one of my biggest emotional breakthroughs. The moment I wrote about was something that occurred 12 years before and that I thought I'd completely gotten over, but it wasn't until I thoroughly examined the moment that I was able to finally let it go.

Knowing how much the assignment helped me and every other person in our writing group, I offer this same assignment to friends. Nearly everyone brave enough to attempt the exercise reported that they gained a lot from it. Although the stories are painful to write and difficult for me to read, I love hearing how much the writing has helped others get past moments that had been eating at them.

This type of writing is one of the cheapest and most accessible forms of therapy. It's also one of the quickest ways to heal emotional pain and has proven effective for many different conditions or mental illnesses. Some of these are PTSD, anxiety, depression, obsessive compulsive disorder, grief and loss, chronic illness issues, substance abuse, eating disorders, interpersonal relationship issues, communication skill issues, and low self-esteem.

If you're interested in doing your own directed writing, pick a moment you want to write about or find a list of prompts to choose from online.

###

Back in 2017, Anthony Johnson and I would regularly train yoga and jiu jitsu four or five days a week. One day after a rough session,

TBI or CTE: What the Hell is Wrong with Me?

Anthony suggested we jump in my pool, which was around 56 degrees. He said the guys he trained with at the Los Angeles Jiu Jitsu Club would do that after their workouts and see how long they could stay in the cold water. He mentioned the documentary *Choke* in which jiu jitsu and MMA legend Rickson Gracie enters a river in Japan and breathes to remain calm in the ice-cold water.

I hadn't seen the movie but said it sounded cool. Not something I could see myself doing but pretty badass.

Anthony jumped in the pool and came up calm. He said it was pretty damn cold, but it didn't seem to be bothering him much. He warned me to go in slowly.

But I'd just watched him jump in and he was fine. So I jumped. And I came up gasping for air, unable to breathe.

Anthony stayed calm but concerned and kept reminding me to breathe, that I was okay.

That jolt scared me. It also embarrassed me. Anthony's about 20 years younger than me and my main training partner. If he could do something, I wanted to prove I could, too. Plus, it'd be nice to have a new challenge, something to distract me from my problems.

The next day I went back into the pool, but just to my waist. I stayed in for a couple of minutes while wondering why anyone would want to do this. I did this every day, and every day I'd go a little longer or deeper. After two months I was able to swim more than 30 minutes in the 52-degree water.

When Anthony saw my interest in the cold, he suggested I watch the Vice documentary on "The Iceman" Wim Hof. Wim, an ordinary looking middle-aged man, was accomplishing extraordinary feats and had several Guinness World Records at the time. One was the farthest swim under ice at 188.6 feet. Another for the fastest half marathon run barefoot on ice and snow. He'd also held the record for the longest time in direct, full-body contact with ice.

Although there were a lot of critics of Wim, including my wife, who assumed he had to be a quack or freak of nature, I didn't care. I witnessed Wim's feats and watched him take nonathletic men and women through incredible experiences such as gathering in nearly frozen lakes and walking up massive snowbound mountains while wearing only shoes, socks, shorts, and a shirt for the women. Joining one of his expeditions went on my hope-to-do-one-day list.

My time exposing myself to the cold faded when winter arrived, but I picked it up again in October, doing the occasional dip in the pool and taking cold showers. The following year was the same pattern with the addition of a ten-day Wim Hof class on the Commune app. By the end of the class, I felt comfortable in the cold, and when my family visited the mountains, I had them bury me in the snow up to my neck wearing just pants and a thin shirt, for a few minutes.

Every year I played with cold immersion, I ended up abandoning it when the weather grew warmer. I liked how the cold made me feel alive and built my mental toughness, but it is not an easy thing to force yourself to do. We're creatures of habit and it's easy to fall into our comfortable ones, like nice warm relaxing showers.

In November 2020, I decided to give the cold immersion another shot, but I found it harder than ever before even though the pool was in the 60s. Instead of caving and putting the cold to the side, I dedicated myself to it as research for the book. Perhaps if I understood why the cold was helping me, I'd be more likely to keep up the practice. I purchased *The Wim Hof Method: Activate Your Full Human Potential* by Wim Hof with the hope I'd find inspiration.

The book is very well-written and easy to understand with specific directions on how to do both the breathwork and cold exposure. It also lists the scientific studies he's been part of and the benefits of the practice.

Like most people, I was aware of the cold's anti-inflammatory effects, and my practice had taught me how great it is for helping to manage emotion. A few minutes in my pool and all my worries went away, whether anxiety, depression, or feeling overwhelmed, and I'd experience a state of calm. I was also aware both my mood and energy levels skyrocketed after daily doses of cold.

In addition to the benefits I knew about, I learned that frequent exposure to cold can speed up metabolism, help with focus, and improve the immune response and quality of sleep. One of the reasons cold exposure is so powerful is the way it stimulates the vascular system. The cold activates and exercises the millions of muscles in the system, and after ten days of exposure, most people will experience a reduction in heart rate and stress. The longer you do the practice, the more control you'll have over your body, your vascular system automatically closing up when entering the cold, avoiding the pain and discomfort that everyone experiences at the beginning.

The book points out that it isn't necessary to spend much time in the cold and the benefits will come at any temperature under 60 degrees. Wim encourages people to begin with 30-second cold showers at the end of a warm shower. The following week, the cold shower is increased to a minute. Add another 30 seconds the third week and again the fourth week and your vascular tone will be optimized. The practice doesn't need to be done every day, but he suggests doing it at least five days a week.

The daily showers, along with the occasional dip in the pool, toughened me up and when January hit, I did 23 days in my pool, averaging 12 minutes a session, most of that time submerged to my chin. Halfway through the sessions I had a huge realization that I no longer looked at the exercise as torture. My body and mind were accustomed to the cold and I could enter the water without hesitation, achieving a sense of calm very quickly.

Not content with the pool only reaching the low 50s and worried it wouldn't properly prep me for one of Wim's expeditions once the pandemic waned and the world opened back up, I figured it was time to try a real ice bath. I'd attempted one the prior year in my bathtub, but I didn't last long at all. This time I was determined to do it right, so I contacted Joey Hauss, a local Level-2 Certified Wim Hof Method instructor, and set up a one-on-one session for the end of February.

Although I wasn't very interested in the breathwork that Joey offered and was only drawn to the videos of men and women stepping calmly into his portable ice bath, I signed up for his Tuesday online breathwork session in the hope it would help me get ready. I'd been doing daily 15- to 20-minute pool plunges the first half of February but was still intimidated by going into water 15 degrees colder than I was used to.

When Joey and his wife stopped by for the session, I learned that it was Joey who had introduced Anthony to the cold pool dips and the reason I began this practice. Joey and his friend Eric, both black belts under Jean Jacques Machado, ran the Los Angeles Jiu Jitsu Club and had been working on developing their cold exposure and breathwork.

Joey, a soft-spoken badass, was a high school and college wrestler and US Marine Sergeant before discovering jiu jitsu. He developed an interest in breathwork and cold exposure while attending a Rickson Gracie seminar. As someone obsessed with finding things that were challenging, Joey dove headfirst into the practice, finding direction when he discovered Wim Hof, who was teaching the scientific community the health and psychological benefits of doing the same types of exercises Joey and Eric were already doing.

TBI or CTE: What the Hell is Wrong with Me?

While Joey and I were setting up for the breathwork session in the backyard, I admitted I was nervous about the ice bath. I hadn't been in the pool for more than a week and wasn't sure how I would do. He said that most people who go to his workshops don't think they can do the ice bath but they almost all do. He told me not to stress over it and assured me that the breath session would prepare me for the dip. "Don't suffer from an ice bath you haven't taken yet."

Thirty minutes later, the breathwork was finished and it was time for the ice bath. Joey stepped in first, his face showing nothing but peace as he sat in the 35-degree water and calmly talked to us, letting me know what to expect.

When it was my turn, I stepped in and sat down on the exhale, thrilled it wasn't very different from the pool. My wrists and hands began to hurt a little after the minute mark, but I hung in for the full two minutes, which is what Joey suggests for the first time. My next ice bath I'll aim to stay in for five minutes with ten being my max goal.

As glad as I was to get through the experience, I admitted to Joey that the ice bath was a bit of a letdown, not because it wasn't what I expected, but because it paled in comparison to what I had received from the breathwork and guided meditation.

Joey laughed and told me about the famous quote in the self-development world. "Sell them what they want to give them what they need."

Chapter Twelve

When my buddy Eugene heard I was gearing up for an ice bath, he suggested I read *Breath* by James Nestor. A book on breathing sounded pretty boring, but I ordered it because Eugene has been a constant source of great advice and encouragement.

Nestor is a journalist who lived a life full of respiratory problems and needed to treat his failing lungs, which had been weakened by several bouts of pneumonia. His doctor recommended Nestor to try a specific breathing technique, the session so powerful that Nestor decided to explore different types of breathing. His first experience is detailed in his book *Deep*, in which he describes travelling to Greece where he interviewed free divers to understand how these men and women could train themselves to hold their breath for up to 12 minutes.

On Nestor's journey around the world, he discovered that mankind has lost the ability to breathe correctly, and this causes a myriad of problems. In *Breath,* he recounts his experiences trying different breathing techniques, which include the Wim Hof Method (a form of the ancient practice called Tummo). Nestor shares his experiences and points to the science, showing how these practices can boost athletic performance, stop asthma and autoimmune disease, and straighten scoliotic spines, to name a few of the benefits. He also makes quite clear the importance of breathing through the nose.

I'd only associated the nose with smelling, and, because mine is always congested, even that ability has been limited. I hadn't considered how the nose adds warmth and moisture to inhaled air for smoother entry to the lungs and assists in filtering allergens and foreign bodies. It also allows for more oxygen to get to active tissues and can increase rest, recovery, and digestion.

TBI or CTE: What the Hell is Wrong with Me?

I've been a mouth breather all my life, but I had no idea how much it was hurting me, especially its contribution to my bearlike snoring. Nestor's suggestion to sleep with lips taped shut sounded strange and uncomfortable since my nose is always clogged before bed, even after using saline rinses to help clear it out. I wasn't very hopeful I'd be able to fall asleep with the tape on, but it actually wasn't an issue. Not only did the tape stop me from snoring, but I woke feeling incredibly rested, more than I could remember at any other time.

Reading the book and practicing nose breathing throughout the day reminded me how I had first learned it from Anthony Johnson. At the time I didn't understand the health benefits of breathing through my nose, only that it helped me get through difficult yoga sessions and improved my cardio in jiu jitsu.

The combination of yoga, the occasional Wim Hof breathing, and a love for challenging myself helped me develop a low-level breathing practice for the past five years. Some days it would mean holding my breath for two minutes at a time. Other days, I'd focus on very long and slow exhales while sitting in the sauna. Often before bed, I'd put myself to sleep by intentionally slowing my breathing down so much it would worry my wife.

But even though I had an attraction to breathwork and *Breath* was teaching me just how powerful the different types of breathing could be, I wasn't excited about doing a weekly online breathwork session with Joey Hauss. Mornings are when I knock out as much work as possible while my son is upstairs doing his distance learning. Lying on a mat doing absolutely nothing but breathing wasn't appealing.

Joey understood why I struggled with taking the time for breathwork and said that is a common point of view with the go-go-go type of men and women who think that if they're not being productive, they're not being useful. Joey suggested what's needed is a perspective change. "Because the truth is that you're doing something very productive," he said. "You may not be moving from point A to point B physically, but you are doing it internally."

He assured me that when you're taking the time to meditate or do breathwork, you're taking the time to better yourself. "In addition to the calmness and peace of mind, your body will function better and have less health problems," Joey said. "It lets you be in a state of flow where you get a lot more done with a lot less effort needing to be put forward."

I wasn't sold on the practice, but I promised to give it a fair shot. The first half of Joey's classes focus on breathing mechanics: using the diaphragm, chest, ribs, and back, hitting each spot separately and then altogether. While surprised there were ways to breathe I wasn't aware of, I found it very difficult to force myself to relax and stop thinking about all the things I could be getting accomplished.

Whatever guilt I had about not being productive had melted away by the end of this breathing, my mind calm and body relaxed. And then it was time for the Wim Hof Method breathing. For the first of four rounds, we fully inhaled through the belly and let it go, creating a circular flow for about 30 breaths. After letting go of the last breath, we held for about a minute, then inhaled as deeply as we could and held it for 30 seconds. When we let that breath go, we started the next round, extending the amount of time holding the breath each of the four rounds.

Although I'd done this type of breathing before, it had been a while and I probably took it further than I had previously. Joey had warned that we might experience tetany, which is increased neuronal excitability that might result in tingling or numbness, often in the hands. I experienced it in my face with both cheeks and my jaw feeling electric. The feeling was interesting but passed while I lay there, and by the end of the session I felt incredible.

This type of conscious heavy breathing stimulates the sympathetic nervous system and has proven to be helpful in reducing stress, improving sleep and sports performance, and adding to focus and clarity. I can testify I had similar results during Joey's other online sessions, always feeling better coming out than I did going in.

It was the in-person session before the ice bath that had the most profound effect on me. Because Joey was there to monitor me and make sure I was safe, we were able to push my limits a bit and go deeper with the breathing. The first half of the session grounded me and helped me relax before we began the Wim Hof Method. The first two rounds were similar to what we had done online, but the final two rounds we kicked up the breathing to double, triple, and quadruple the rate of breathing with breath retention reaching two minutes.

At the completion of the breathing, Joey instructed me to lie there and relax while music played. Relaxing was hard because I was examining the intense feeling of a million butterflies fluttering on my chest. I also could not stop the involuntary shaking ripping through my body, but Joey kept reminding me that the shaking was normal and to let it happen. The shaking lasted through the four minutes of the song, and I was in such a different place mentally when Joey began the guided meditation portion of his practice.

While the breathwork with Joey was amazing, I was surprised by how much I responded to his guided meditation. I'd read how much meditation can help people manage their emotions, but just like breathing, I'd found meditation to be boring and not something I'd care to do. I wasn't even going to mention it in the book until taking Joey's class and realizing I'd be doing myself and my readers a huge disservice by not including it.

#

Damn it. It's mid-April and I'm only now writing this section. The plan had been to read a book or two on meditation and to meditate every day in March.

I failed at both goals even though I purchased *Level Up 108*, the follow up to Travis Eliot's *Ultimate Yogi*, which I've practiced to hundreds of times over the last seven years. I purchased it because of the meditation classes you are encouraged to do each day, just like the yoga. Unfortunately, I couldn't get myself to do any. Well, I did do one, but I did it at my desk. And I might have checked an email or two while the class was playing. Possibly looked to see who liked my last post. Saw no one had. Got depressed.

See, that meditation shit doesn't work.

I told myself I didn't need to do the meditation classes anyway because I was already getting so much from the yoga. The combination of the breathwork, Travis's calming voice, and the nuggets of wisdom throughout the classes put me in a better place mentally. I was more relaxed. At peace. It was plenty.

It would be easy to make this the shortest section in the book by saying meditation wasn't for me but that that you should do it because of X, Y, and Z. The truth is that I'm tired of working on this project. I'm burned out reading nonfiction and trying out different techniques. What I want is time to write my novels and short stories, all put on hold so I can just sit still and breathe and do what feels like nothing.

Hating to be called a quitter, I decided I'd give meditation one last try, but a real attempt with no distractions. I set the infrared sauna to 140 degrees and laid down the towels, lit up my vaporizer and got high, holding that last hit a minute thanks to my improved lung capacity. (Thanks Joey!)

My last online breathing session I did sober in the sauna, and it was awesome. The sauna is where I do some of my best self-reflection, often sitting in silence for the first 15 to 20 minutes whether sober or high on cannabis. I never thought of this time as meditating, but that's exactly what it is, a time for going internal and focusing on breath. I'd been doing that for so long it was just part of my routine.

I picked the *Body Scan* meditation from the *Level Up 108* program because the name implied I would be doing something. I sat upright in a comfortable position, began deep, slow breathing through my nose and did my best to follow Travis's instructions to visualize different body parts while internally repeating "May you be healthy."

My tough guy ego came roaring in, saying that this was foolish, ridiculous even, to wish a body part healthy by bathing it with positive energy. That was one of the problems I was having while reading *Becoming Supernatural* by Dr. Joe Dispenza. Even though he shows the science and power of meditation, my conditioning makes it hard to accept that meditation is much more than wishful thinking.

Perhaps I shall meditate tomorrow on why that is.

But I stopped that voice and thanked him for his input, said I was still determined to give it a try. I focused on my breath and did what Travis said, wished every inch of my body healthy. It didn't matter whether I believed it was going to work, I just did it, and by the end of the 10-minute meditation I felt so much better than when I went in.

Yes, part of my euphoria was due to being high, but I'm high nine days out of ten and I know it wasn't just that. And true, just the breathwork would have put me in a better place, which is why it's a powerful part of any meditative practice.

The breathwork is what made my guided meditations with Joey so powerful. The breathing primes the body and puts the brain in a more receptive state to accept new information.

"During the breathwork you also go into different parts of your brain," Joey said. "Your prefrontal cortex starts quieting down so all the mental chatter goes away. You start going deeper into reptilian, mammalian parts of the brain. A lot of times people have these emotional releases because so much is stored in our mammalian brain."

Instead of picking up the stack of papers beside me in the sauna and being productive, I decided to do nothing and put on another meditation.

Mental Noting. The class begins with Travis saying, "Meditation has sometimes been described as making friends with that crazy person inside your head. And in this meditation we're going to get to practice that."

After a quick intro and body scan, I was already back in a meditative state and feeling terrific. The goal was to keep my focus on my breath. Every time a new thought came up, I would note it and go back to my anchor.

At one point, Travis mentioned you might notice sounds, and a few seconds later my backyard gate opened. I noted it and let it go, wasn't bothered in the least that a serial killer might have just slipped onto my property with the intent to slaughter us.

Hearing a sound and letting it go was something I was good at. Some might attribute that to old age, marriage, or kids, but I give credit to Anthony Johnson, who'd taught me that in our yoga sessions. In fact, just as Joey began the guided meditation in my backyard, my neighbor cranked on his leaf blower. Joey turned up the music, but the leaf blower overpowered it. Instead of being upset about the noise, I smiled knowing I could tune it out.

When *Mental Noting* ended, I felt incredible and was hit with the revelation that I'd been cheating myself out of something great. I had read many articles recommending meditation. Scott McQuary and Michael Poorman both swore by it. Why not add in a meditation every day, especially if I'm going to go into the sauna to breathe anyway? Why not make the experience even better?

Drenched in sweat, my mind and body baking, I put on a third meditation, truly testing myself with *Loving Kindness*.

This class called for me to visualize a person that symbolizes love in my life. I chose my mother and played along, wishing her, "May you be healthy, may you be happy, may you be at peace."

The next set of instructions guided the listener to become that person, to look at oneself through their eyes, and to imagine how they felt. From my mother's viewpoint, I saw myself smiling and sending love, and I knew how wonderful that would make her feel. If anyone else asks I'll swear it was sweat, but between you and me, I may have shed a tear or two.

At the end of the meditation, I was in full-blown bliss. Although I had set the sauna for an hour, I got out 20 minutes early and started writing. Not only had the meditating been beneficial for my body and mind, but also removed a huge writer's block I'd been struggling with. It reminded me of Travis's saying, "By doing nothing, everything begins to happen."

The next day, I got the meditation out of the way first thing in the morning. Thirty minutes after waking, and sober, I went into the sauna and played *Level Up*. The meditating didn't come easy, my mind too distracted with the thought of noting any reaction so I could include it in this book. It was still a good exercise in bringing myself back into focus.

Instead of stopping, I realized I wanted more of the feeling I'd had the previous day. I put on *Mental Noting* to chase the high, doubting I wouldn't achieve it. But a few minutes in, I was grinning, feeling incredible, like my head was filled with beautiful white light.

On Sunday, I stuck with the same routine and went with the *Presence* meditation. The instructions were to keep saying the word "presence" to bring you back to the moment, but every time Travis said it, my brain went straight to Christmas. Presents, presents, presents. And I wasn't even high. But I still finished the meditation feeling better than I had before the session, grateful I could smile about my distracted brain and not be the least bit upset with myself for not doing the meditation correctly. It was ten minutes well spent.

That night, my wife told me that for the last few days I'd been different, but in a good way. She said I seemed so much happier, lighter, that I was smiling a lot and having more fun.

I hated to admit it but said it was most likely because of the meditation. As corny as it sounded, doing nothing was paying off.

The rest of the week, I finished the other meditations, ending on *Gratitude*, during which Travis says, "When gratitude appears, all negativity disappears."

While I managed to feel gratitude for a few people and things, this class was only a fraction as powerful as the backyard session with Joey in which he turned me into a gratitude vacuum and had me reconsider moments I had always viewed negatively. The experience permanently changed the way I perceived a few major life events and left me filled with gratitude.

"Gratitude, forgiveness, appreciation, love—they're not just these mental constructs," Joey said. "They are these physical reactions and feelings in the body. It feels a certain way when you actively forgive someone. It feels a certain way when you're grateful for a thing. And there's a big difference between thinking you're happy and actively feeling it in your body."

So even though I might always have a hang-up regarding traditional meditation and the language used, I now understand just how good it makes me feel and that I want more of it. In addition to doing Joey's weekly online sessions, I plan on trying out all the Inner Dimensions meditation classes and will continue to use those that serve me best. Meditation will be another tool to help me live a healthier and happier life.

I'm leaving out the science about meditation because I realize it's not the books or knowledge that persuade me to continue or stop therapy techniques. I really don't care how things work and only want to know how they make me feel. If it makes me feel good, then I'm going to want to do more of it. If I don't enjoy it, I'll skip it and find something else.

It's all about discovering what works best for you. If you want to know exactly why meditation works, then dig up some books on that. If you want to start experimenting, there is no shortage of free guided meditations on the internet, and you're sure to find something that resonates with you. Perhaps it's a man's voice, maybe a woman's, or you might prefer just music. Maybe you are ready for more than that and just need silence to run through your own meditation. If you can add a form of conscious breathing to it, that's even better.

Being present, being conscious, being mindful. Many describe that state as heaven on Earth and what we should strive for. I encourage you to give it a shot because, honestly, how would you be more productive with those ten minutes?

#

It's finally time to address the big gray smoldering elephant in the room. That's right, let's take a look at my cannabis use along with the pros and cons of using the substance, a conversation I have with myself on a regular basis. And by regular basis, I mean daily. At least since I began writing this book and was forced to take an honest look at myself.

I'm not here to glorify or condone the plant, but it's been the most consistent of my coping mechanisms since I began piling up traumatic brain injuries. I won't claim I only use cannabis because of the TBIs and resulting symptoms, but my heaviest usage does coincide with the years I was involved in football, MMA, and boxing, and the aftermath of that damage.

My first experience with cannabis was during my sophomore year in high school when I was at a party with my buddy Marc. We were both on the small side and had been getting the shit kicked out of us in football practice. We'd also been drinking fairly heavily for the past year. After that first time, I was always on the lookout, trying to figure out who else smoked and could get hold of it. If we were lucky, we might be able to get high on the weekends. A year later and I was smoking whenever possible. By my senior year it was nearly daily.

My use dropped a bit the first two years out of high school when I wasn't playing football, but I became a religious smoker at Brown, spending much of my time there high when I wasn't lifting weights or practicing. There were a few years after college when I only smoked occasionally, but once I began fighting, I was using cannabis daily, generally at night to also help me sleep. Although I did make some bad decisions while high, I'm sure I've made just as many sober, and probably ten times as many when drunk.

One of the biggest reasons I love cannabis is that it has significantly enhanced my creativity. Except for a few small breaks, everything I've written, including this book, has come from that place. I never wanted it to be a crutch, something that I needed to have in order to write; but if cannabis helps speed up the process and put me in the zone that's most ideal for me to create, then why not use it?

Legality and morality are two of the reasons people might point to for not using cannabis. Although cannabis is currently legal in California, it wasn't for the first 25 years I was using. It has also been illegal on the federal level since 1937; and in 1970 the Feds categorized it as a Schedule 1 drug, meaning it was considered to have no acceptable medical use and was part of the class of drugs, along with heroin, considered to have the highest potential for abuse.

TBI or CTE: What the Hell is Wrong with Me?

I'm not going into the questionable reasons why cannabis was outlawed in the first place, but I will say the Schedule 1 categorization and the government's claim that they want to protect us are ludicrous. What about alcohol? How about cigarettes? Fast food? Diet soda? It's not about our health.

Now that states are finally legalizing cannabis, does that change whether it's moral to use it? How can something be wrong to do one day and totally fine the next, just because lawmakers said so? That has never made any sense to me and has never been a consideration in how I live my life.

Since I began a journal for this book three years ago, I've had one 40-day break, two five-day breaks, and a few days here and there where I didn't get high. Let's say 55 days off out of the last 1,100. And that's with Dr. Alison Gordon telling me I should take off seven days in a row once a month.

Looking at that journal is a great way to see how much my cannabis usage has decreased, even if the number of days doesn't reflect that. The hormone regulation that is part of Dr. Gordon's protocol cut my use in half, making it so I didn't need to use it throughout the day. The combination of NUCCA and neurofeedback cut that amount in half once again, and for the past year I rarely use cannabis before 5 p.m. and nowhere near the amount I had been using.

Therapy sessions with Mark Harris helped me understand why I was using cannabis and whether it should be considered an addiction; the main question was if it negatively impacted my life. Although self-assessments are obviously biased, I had many talks with my wife to help me examine my cannabis use, and we always came up with the same answer, that, for me, it was much more beneficial than harmful.

When I use cannabis, I become very self-reflective, and one of the first things I do is apologize to my family for anything I could have done differently during the day. Whether it was how I talked to them or something I could have done better, the cannabis helps me take a better look at myself.

The cannabis also helped me a great deal with my anxiety, depression, and emotional stability, my three biggest problems associated with TBIs. Cannabis consistently lifts my mood and significantly lowers physical pain. And because I stick to strains that have energy-inducing effects, the cannabis doesn't negatively affect my work and generally increases productivity. I have to remind you that very little research has been done on the benefits and health risks of this Schedule 1 drug, so please do your own digging to see what you believe is true. It is up to each individual to research potential side effects.

The most concerning thing I've read about the long-term effects of cannabis use was in Dr. Amen's *The End of Mental Illness*. In 2016, Dr. Amen and his colleagues released a study of more than 1,000 cannabis users that showed that nearly every part of their brains was lower in blood flow volume than in the brains of nonusers. Blood flow was noticeably decreased in the right hippocampus, which is associated with Alzheimer's and memory loss.[2]

Two years later, they published the largest brain imaging study to date, which showed cannabis was associated with accelerated brain aging. They found that cannabis use caused 2.8 years of accelerated aging while alcohol accounted for only 0.6 year.[3]

Even with this knowledge, I've chosen to continue using it. Partly because we're going to die anyway, so why not live the best life possible. If my daily life is improved by cannabis, then I'm

---

[2] Daniel G. Amen et al., "Discriminative Properties of Hippocampal Hypoperfusion in Marijuana Users Compared to Healthy Controls: Implications for Marijuana Administration in Alzheimer's Dementia," *Journal of Alzheimer's Disease* 56, no.1 (2017) 261-73

[3] Daniel G. Amen et al., "Patterns of Regional Cerebral Blood Flow as a Function of Age throughout the Lifespan" *Journal of Alzheimer's Disease* 65, no.4 (2018): 1087-92

TBI or CTE: What the Hell is Wrong with Me?

okay paying the price at the end. It's also incredibly hard to talk myself out of something when I've functioned so well with it, including the testing I underwent at the Cleveland Clinic and at Vital Head and Spinal Care, not to mention the hundreds of interviews I've conducted while high.

Although I didn't do any sober testing at the Cleveland Clinic to compare against results from tests I took high, I did do so near the end of my neurofeedback training at Vital Head and Spinal Care. In the first image I was sober and hadn't used cannabis for 12 hours. The second image is from two weeks later when I was quite high after consuming 40 mg of sativa an hour before the test. (Image at back of book Testing and Scans)

The IVA-2 results show my attention went up a bit, but my response control declined. The increase in hyperactivity was also enough to put me back in the ADHD range.

One of the other reasons I've had trouble kicking the habit is that every time I stop, I become a little more irritable and restless and have trouble sleeping. Feeling guilty I haven't been following doctors' orders, and figuring it'd help me write this section, I just completed a four-day break. Yes, it was supposed to be seven, but I'm a pro at rationalizing my addictions and decided to cut it short.

Because I was worried about becoming too irritable without THC, I did use CBD at night, which is the nonpsychoactive part of cannabis that offers many beneficial properties, including neuroprotective, anti-inflammatory and antianxiety without the high. But even with the CBD, the first two nights of sleep were terrible. The third night was better and by the fourth night my sleep was back to normal.

Despite the bad sleep, I managed to remain in a good mood throughout the day, never feeling the need for cannabis. When my usual light-up time rolled around, I wasn't very tempted to use it and I didn't feel as if I was missing much. Sure, it made video game time with my wife a little less fun, but I also ate fewer late-night snacks.

Last night, I made the decision to break my break. I didn't use as much as usual, but it did put me in a better mood. It was nice realizing the cannabis wasn't really making much of a difference either way, and there is a chance I won't use it as frequently from now on.

Part of me feels that I should abandon cannabis and stick with CBD, along with doing yoga, meditation, breathwork, and cold exposure for the mood enhancement. I wish I had the willpower of Wim Hof, who says, "Get high on your own supply," but I can be lazy and want that immediate fix. I also like intensifying those positive experiences with cannabis, and worry over losing my creative edge is something I need to consider.

Finally, a word of caution. I am not a scientist, doctor, health expert, or role model. I'm just a guy trying to find his best way through life, and what works for me doesn't mean it will do the same for you. Do your own research and make your own decisions to achieve an exceptional life.

Chapter Thirteen

I didn't originally consider including psychedelics in this book. But I changed my mind after reading Michael's Pollan's book *How to Change Your Mind* and countless articles about the studies showing the promising results of psychedelics on brain health. I'd had limited experience with the subject, but my one DMT (N, N-Dimethyltryptamine) trip was absolutely incredible, one of the most beautiful experiences I've ever had.

Because I was still undergoing neurofeedback, I asked Dr. Licata his opinion about the benefits of psychedelics. While he agreed that psychedelics had great potential, he reminded me about my impulsivity and the temptation to throw everything I could at my brain. Dr. Licata said my brain needed time to gradually rehab and make positive changes permanent, and he repeated what Pollan had mentioned in the book, that there is a risk for those with brain health issues who use psychedelics.

Smart enough to take Dr. Licata's advice, I spent the last year and a half reshaping myself into a much happier and healthier person in both body and mind. It wasn't until I began the breathwork and cold exposure with Joey Hauss that psychedelics came back in view. While discussing Joey's path and upcoming self-improvement book, he talked about how much plant-based medicine helped him. I asked him to devise a plan I could follow.

First, I was going to do a heavy dose of cannabis edibles. A few days later, I would do magic mushrooms (psilocybin). The third trip would be LSD, the fourth DMT, and the finishing touch would be ayahuasca.

Just as I was scheduling these experiences, I realized I wanted to do them for the wrong reasons. As hard as it was to admit, this psychedelic adventure was to have fun and explore my mind, not because I wanted to see how they would help my TBI symptoms which are at an all-time low.

Due to the cost, the time to do the research and writing, the risk involved in obtaining the psychedelics, and the small risk presented in consuming them, I decided not to include the subject in this book. I will probably do my exploration, as I believe it is worthwhile for people to research psychedelics as a potentially powerful tool.

I had also planned to write about acupuncture and sensory deprivation float sessions because both modalities work well for me and help with mood elevation and stability. As I mentioned in a previous chapter, I was tempted to do a SPECT scan at the Amen Clinic and to try out the hyperbaric oxygen treatment (HBOT) that Dr. Amen recommends for TBI.

There were quite a few other things I had wanted to discuss in this book and ended up leaving out due to cost, time, lack of availability thanks to COVID-19, and the realization that there is only so much we can do for ourselves. We absolutely need to be proactive, but once we obtain a satisfying brain health level, we should focus on maintaining it. I will always be doing something for my brain, but the quest to improve even more is over.

Being my own worst critic, I must remind myself that this isn't me being lazy or unfocused. It's about doing what is right for my overall health and mental well-being. Continually trying to improve one area of my life by neglecting others isn't what I want. I desire balance, and a big part of that balance is returning to my fiction, my true passion, which has been largely neglected because of this project.

I also want to put this book behind me so I can focus on enjoying life. Today, we celebrated my son's eighth birthday and had a great day. While pretending to be a shark swimming after Jake and his friends, I thought of Michael Poorman's daughter,

TBI or CTE: What the Hell is Wrong with Me?

O'Shen, who recommended, "Enjoy the good days, because you never know how many you might have." I did a lot of reflecting today, flashing back to crying in the backyard, fighting with my wife, losing my shit watching videos of boxers with battered brains, slowly coming to terms with the fact that I had brain damage because I put myself in dangerous situations. It's hard to imagine being that miserable version of myself, and I can't help wondering where I'd be if I hadn't started the journey, if I hadn't questioned whether I was as fine as I thought I was.

I'm not being melodramatic when I say I don't know how I would have gotten through this pandemic if it weren't for everything I've done. There's no telling what might have happened, but the odds are I would've wound up dead, divorced, or in prison, most definitely in a much worse place than I am now.

So despite complaining about the time taken and the emotional toll of writing this book, I'll be forever grateful that I underwent this process.

I'm incredibly grateful to Brian Esquivel for first bringing brain damage to my attention and warning me that I was getting the shit kicked out of me by athletes half my age. Also, I appreciate him turning me on to Dr. Mark Gordon through the Joe Rogan Experience podcast episode.

None of this would have been possible if it weren't for my wife, Jen, who supported my decision to write this book and encouraged and loved me in my darkest moments.

I'm thankful for my sister, Mary, who has been involved in the creation of this book from the start and who had recommended I check out Vital Head and Spinal Care. Not only did that play a huge part in my recovery, but it also led to my mother's incredible turnabout, hopefully preventing her from developing dementia.

I really appreciate Russell Longo for pointing me in the right direction at the start of this project and giving me hope that the brain could be changed in a positive direction.

Sincere thanks go out to all the doctors and friends that have helped me rehab my brain and heal my body. I also appreciate all the books and apps that have made learning and trying new things so much easier.

I'm also grateful for all of the people that have written to me over the past few years, confiding how traumatic brain injuries had altered their life. In addition to Michael Poorman and Scott McQuary, who opened their lives and homes to me, I've had people from across the world write to me about their brain health and how glad they were I was chronicling my recovery. These are the people I've been writing this book for, especially after I reached a stable emotional level and felt that I didn't need to continue the writing.

It's impossible to know how one's own story and words might impact another person, but my wish is that you get some of the same benefits reading this book that I had in researching and writing it.

The most important step is taking an honest assessment of yourself. Really consider who you are, where you are mentally, and whether your idea of being fine or normal matches your evaluation. This includes asking friends and family members to evaluate you as well and ask how they would rate you and your symptoms.

Remember to look at your brain health through the three windows Dr. Licata pointed out: biochemical, mental health, and physical. We are complex creatures and it's important not to neglect any part.

Accept what Dr. Alison Gordon told me, that the quest for brain health is a journey and not a one-stop-one-pill fix. Just as you need to care for your body or it will deteriorate, your brain requires consistent care.

Realize the importance of exercise, sleep, and nutrition and make a commitment to improve these to the best of your ability. Understand that the only real way to know where your brain stands, is by testing it with a functional imaging study like a SPECT scan or qEEG. Testing your hormones and emotional responses is equally important.

Be okay with not being the best at the new activities, hobbies, and sports that you add to your daily routine. Embrace the challenge of trying something new and try to do it with a childlike interest. Understand it's all about doing the activity, not mastering it.

Don't overwhelm yourself. It's all the small things you do that make a big difference. You don't have to do 90-day programs, 30-day cleanses, practice a language every day. Do as Joey Hauss suggested and keep things manageable and realistic. Find what brings you happiness, calm, and stability and switch things up. I never know how my day is going to go, but I do know I'll squeeze in at least one or two positive things.

Recognize all the positive coping mechanisms that you already have and become aware of the negative ones you can improve. Yoga, breathing, jiu jitsu, cannabis, talking with friends, writing, and doing a podcast—these were all things I did prior to this research that were keeping me somewhat sane without me realizing it.

Be kind to yourself for your past mistakes and move forward while taking responsibility for slipups and asking those you hurt for forgiveness. Trust others, confide in them, and try not to worry about being a burden or scaring them.

Live each day the very best you can. Keep positive. Keep going. This might be the toughest struggle you ever face but get after it. Be proactive. Accept help. Make this life as great as possible.

Even if I do develop CTE or another form of dementia, I've made my peace with that. If it occurs, I will intensify my coping mechanisms and make the most of it. But if all that truly matters is the present moment, both the past and future don't matter. Why be upset about something that may never happen? All I must strive for is a good day today, in this moment. If your day is filled with good moments, then that's a good day. If your life is full of good days, then that's a good life.

If you gained something from this book, I hope you will help spread the word and bring awareness. You may not know who in your life feels like something is off but cannot express what it is. Don't be embarrassed by your personal struggles because the person right next to you may be silently fighting similar demons. Make the world a better place by sharing your story.

As a final reminder, don't forget to watch out for loved ones that are involved in contact sports, accidents, or the military or who have suffered any type of blow to the head or emotional trauma.

May your life be filled with health, happiness, and hope.

The End

REVIEW

If you enjoyed this book, I hope you'll take a moment to write a quick review. As an independent author, word of mouth and reviews are incredibly helpful. Whether you leave one star or five, honest feedback is truly appreciated. And if you're on Goodreads or BookBub please stalk me. I believe the technical term is Follow, but I strive on anxiety and what better way to amp it up than thinking there are thousands of strangers stalking me. Plus, you'll be alerted to all my new books and deals. Sounds like a win-win to me.

To leave a review on Goodreads – https://bit.ly/2EDs2zV
To follow on Bookbub – https://bit.ly/2ZDjMHB
To sign up for my newsletter - https://bit.ly/3qnNX1q
Thank you!

RESOURCES

Here are the different books and websites that I mentioned in the book:
Dr. Norman Doidge – *The Brain That Changes Itself*
Dr. Matthew Walker – *Why We Sleep: Unlocking the Power of Sleep and Dreams*
Dr. Christopher Nowinski - *Head Games*
Dr. Daniel Amen – *The End of Mental Illness*
Wim Hof – *The Wim Hof Method: Activate Your Full Human Potential*
James Nestor – *Breath*
Adrian Raine – *The Anatomy of Violence*

Here are the websites I mentioned:
Concussion Legacy Foundation – https://concussionfoundation.org
Cleveland Clinic - https://my.clevelandclinic.org/

Here are the studies that were noted:
[1] Daniel G. Amen et al., "Discriminative Properties of Hippocampal Hypoperfusion in Marijuana Users Compared to Healthy Controls: Implications for Marijuana Administration in Alzheimer's Dementia," *Journal of Alzheimer's Disease* 56, no.1 (2017) 261-73
[2] Daniel G. Amen et al., "Patterns of Regional Cerebral Blood Flow as a Function of Age throughout the Lifespan" *Journal of Alzheimer's Disease* 65, no.4 (2018): 1087-92

ACKNOWLEDGEMENTS

I would like to thank my editors, Mary Nyeholt and Michael Tullius, for all their help putting this book together. I would have been lost without them and doubt I would have continued this journey if it hadn't been for them.

I'd also like to thank all the doctors and health care professionals that helped me with my research and my recovery.

On these next pages I've included information about each of these groups in the hope they might help you further.

CONCUSSION Legacy Foundation

Pledge to donate your brain:
Join Mark and pledge to donate your brain to the Concussion Legacy Foundation, or sign up to participate in clinical research studies while you are alive. Your participation can help advance our understanding of concussion, CTE, and other consequences of head impacts.

Sign up at PledgeMyBrain.org

Make a gift to support the Concussion Legacy Foundation:
The Concussion Legacy Foundation is leading the fight against concussions and CTE and is dedicated to improving the lives of those impacted. From crucial patient and family resources to research and education programs creating a safer future, your contribution makes a difference.

Support the mission at ConcussionFoundation.org/Give

The Millennium Health Centers Mental Health Program

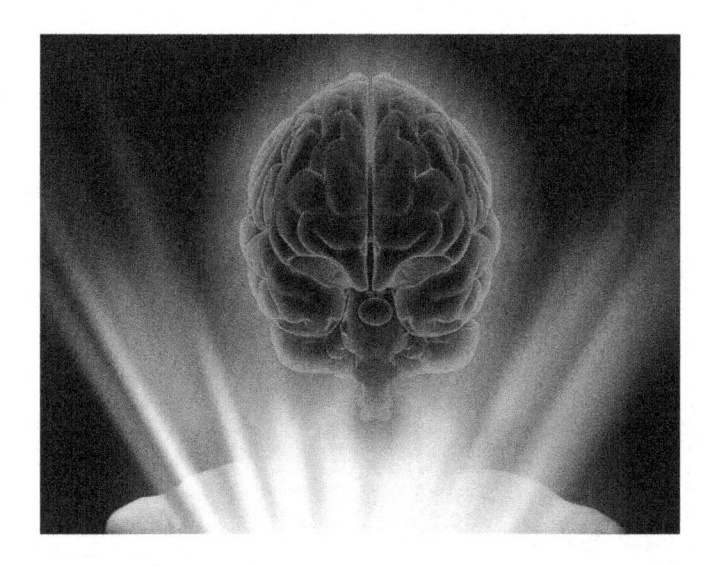

The Millennium protocol played a crucial role in rehabbing my mental health. I highly recommend doctors Mark Gordon and Alison Gordon and believe hormone regulation should be one of your first steps in your healing process.

https://tbihelpnow.org/

Vital Head and Spinal Care

Olivia Tullius, Mark Tullius, Giancarlo Licata, DC, qEEG-D

Train your brain, change your life

You can measurably improve your ADHD, Anxiety, and Memory in 12 weeks so that you can feel better and work smarter…at school and at work.

Our Personal Brain Trainers can use advanced brain tests and neurofeedback technology to help you strengthen your brain to gain focus, reduce anxiety, and prevent memory decline.

https://www.vitalheadandspine.com

WE ARE HERE FOR YOU!

Transforming The Way Mental Health Is Treated

Our brain-based approach goes beyond traditional psychiatry to give you the answers you want and the results you deserve.

Amen Clinics offer a full spectrum of psychiatric services including:

- Comprehensive Brain Health Evaluations
- Brain SPECT Imaging
- Integrative/Functional Medicine
- Nutrition Counseling & Therapy
- Brain Health Coaching
- Hyperbaric Oxygen Therapy (HBOT)
- General Counseling & Therapy

888-288-9834 | www.amenclinics.com

Atlanta | Chicago | Dallas | Los Angeles | New York | Orange County, CA
San Francisco | Seattle | Washington, D.C.

JOEY HAUSS

GET COMFORTABLE BEING UNCOMFORTABLE.

Joey is a Level 2 Certified Wim Hof Method Instructor, Breathwork Facilitator, Black Belt in Brazilian Jiu Jitsu under Jean Jacques Machado and Former US Marine Sergeant.

On a mission to help people become happy, healthy and strong — one state, country and continent at a time.

- LIVE Online Breathwork Session
- Wim Hof Method Workshops
- 1-on-1 Coaching

joeyhauss.com

INNER DIMENSION TV

TRANSFORM YOUR BODY. AWAKEN YOUR SOUL.

ONLINE YOGA | MEDITATION | DAILY WISDOM

Download on the App Store | GET IT ON Google Play

INNERDIMENSIONTV.COM

The Wim Hof Method

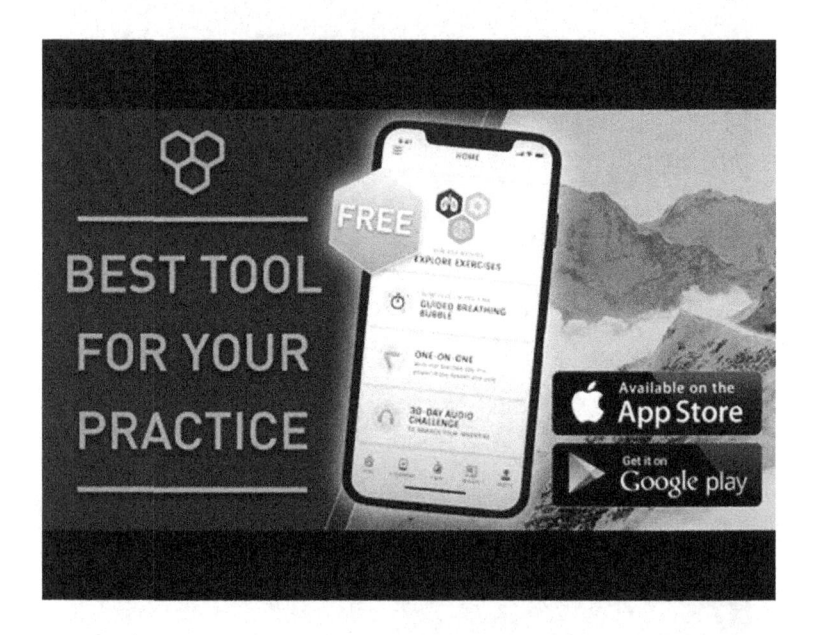

Take Wim with you wherever you go

Intuitive, developed with user feedback, and jam-packed with features, the WHM app is the ultimate companion to your practice. Get the free base version, or subscribe to unlock a wealth of premium features. Download the app from the Apple or Google Play store and start your exercises today!

https://www.wimhofmethod.com

VITAL
Brain & Spine

Dr. Radwanski is the founder and owner of Vital Brain & Spine. She has extensively studied the complexities of the craniocervical junction and the effects that a misalignment has on the brain, leading to dizziness, chronic headaches (often associated with intractable post concussion syndrome), and chronic pain.

NUCCA combines state-of-the-art technology, specific measurements, and gentle, precise corrections.

Her approach yields profound results to overcome your pain.

https://www.vitalbrainandspine.com/

An Important Documentary

This is an excellent documentary that everyone should watch.
https://quietexplosions.com

TESTING AND SCANS

IVA-2 Standard Scale Analysis

Name: Tullius, Mark
Test Date: 8/6/2019 9:32 AM   Age: 46   DOB: 8/19/1972   Sex: M   On Meds: U
Highest Education: Examiner ID: Unknown

FS Attention Quotient = 95

Auditory	Visual
AQ = 81	AQ = 110

Vigilance: 61, Focus: 77, Speed: 118 (Auditory)
Vigilance: 103, Focus: 111, Speed: 109 (Visual)

FS Response Control Quotient = 97

Auditory	Visual
RCQ = 91	RCQ = 104

Prudence: 107, Consistency: 89, Stamina: 85 (Auditory)
Prudence: 107, Consistency: 99, Stamina: 102 (Visual)

Sustained Auditory Attention Quotient = 77   Sustained Visual Attention Quotient = 105

Auditory Response Validity Check: Valid
Visual Response Validity Check: Valid
Attention Factor: Positive   Impulsive Hyperactivity Factor: Positive

IVA-2 Standard Scale Analysis

Name: Tullius, Mark

Test Date: 10/29/2019 11:49 AM **Age:** 47 **DOB:** 8/19/1972 **Sex:** M **On Meds:** U

Highest Education: **Examiner ID:** Unknown

FS Attention Quotient = 107

Auditory	Visual
AQ = 104	AQ = 108

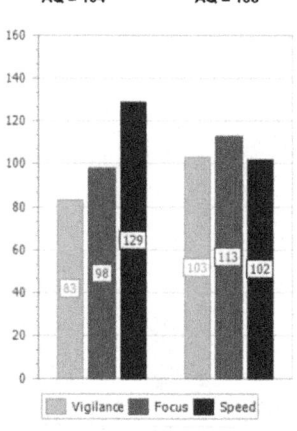

Vigilance: 83, Focus: 98, Speed: 129
Vigilance: 103, Focus: 113, Speed: 102

FS Response Control Quotient = 104

Auditory	Visual
RCQ = 104	RCQ = 103

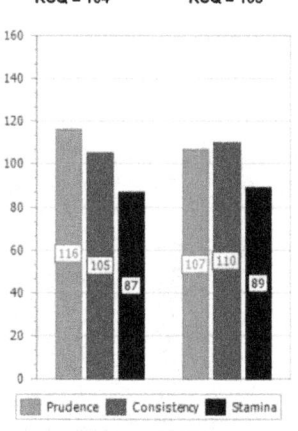

Prudence: 116, Consistency: 105, Stamina: 87
Prudence: 107, Consistency: 110, Stamina: 89

Sustained Auditory Attention Quotient = 104 **Sustained Visual Attention Quotient = 108**

Auditory Response Validity Check: Valid

Visual Response Validity Check: Valid

Attention Factor: Positive **Impulsive Hyperactivity Factor:** Negative

IVA-2 Standard Scale Analysis

Name: Tullius, Mark
Test Date: 12/20/2019 9:59 AM **Age:** 47 **DOB:** 8/19/1972 **Sex:** M **On Meds:** U
Highest Education: **Examiner ID:** Unknown

FS Attention Quotient = 121

Auditory	Visual
AQ = 123	AQ = 117

Vigilance: 105 / 103
Focus: 108 / 123
Speed: 140 / 111

FS Response Control Quotient = 103

Auditory	Visual
RCQ = 96	RCQ = 109

Prudence: 107 / 107
Consistency: 84 / 108
Stamina: 100 / 104

Sustained Auditory Attention Quotient = 122   Sustained Visual Attention Quotient = 112

Auditory Response Validity Check: Valid
Visual Response Validity Check: Valid
Attention Factor: Negative   **Impulsive Hyperactivity Factor:** Negative

Test Date: 1/6/2020 10:56 AM   Age: 47   DOB: 8/19/1972   Sex: M   On Meds: U

Highest Education: Examiner ID: Unknown

FS Attention Quotient = 125

Auditory	Visual
AQ = 127	AQ = 120

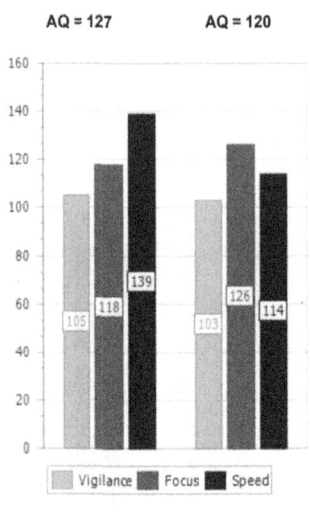

Vigilance 105, Focus 118, Speed 139 (Auditory)
Vigilance 103, Focus 126, Speed 114 (Visual)

FS Response Control Quotient = 118

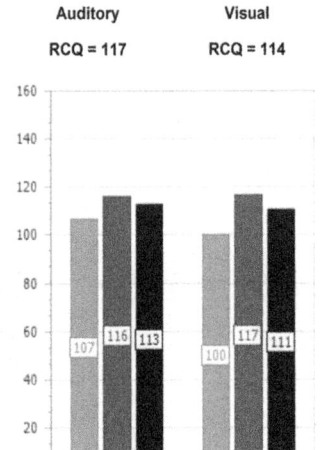

Auditory	Visual
RCQ = 117	RCQ = 114

Prudence 107, Consistency 116, Stamina 113 (Auditory)
Prudence 100, Consistency 117, Stamina 111 (Visual)

Sustained Auditory Attention Quotient = 122   Sustained Visual Attention Quotient = 105

Auditory Response Validity Check: Valid
Visual Response Validity Check: Valid

Attention Factor: Negative   **Impulsive Hyperactivity Factor:** Positive

Traumatic Brain Injury Discriminant Analysis*

TBI DISCRIMINANT SCORE = 1.69   TBI PROBABILITY INDEX = 99.5%

The TBI Probability Index is the subject's probability of membership in the mild traumatic brain injury population. (see Thatcher et al, EEG and Clin. Neurophysiol., 73: 93-106, 1989.)

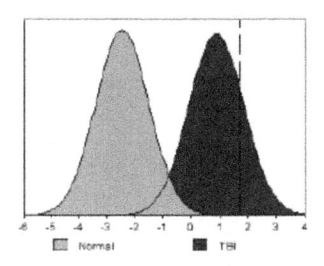

			RAW	Z
FP1-F3	COH	Theta	88.48	0.78
T3-T5	COH	Beta	80.20	1.98
C3-P3	COH	Beta	83.91	0.74
FP2-F4	PHA	Beta	0.07	-1.15
F3-F4	PHA	Beta	-0.06	-1.08
F4-T6	AMP	Alpha	63.36	1.96
F8-T6	AMP	Alpha	47.34	2.74
F4-T6	AMP	Beta	54.10	1.62
F8-T6	AMP	Beta	39.98	2.59
F3-O1	AMP	Alpha	-5.76	1.14
F4-O2	AMP	Alpha	4.54	1.13
F7-O1	AMP	Alpha	31.92	-1.68
F4-O2	AMP	Beta	25.42	1.19
P3	RP	Alpha	22.65	-2.09
P4	RP	Alpha	29.63	-2.33
O1	RP	Alpha	26.56	-2.08
O2	RP	Alpha	23.71	-2.48
T4	RP	Alpha	22.23	-1.68
T5	RP	Alpha	23.29	-2.26
T6	RP	Alpha	21.27	-2.48

TBI SEVERITY INDEX = 4.69

This severity score places the patient in the MODERATE range of severity.

			RAW	Z
FP1-C3	COH	Delta	73.86	1.77
FP1-FP2	COH	Theta	88.26	0.47
O1-P7	COH	Alpha	33.53	0.28
O2-T6	COH	Alpha	77.37	-0.72
P3-O1	COH	Beta	85.06	1.29
FP1-T3	PHA	Theta	-1.05	-0.74
T3-T4	PHA	Theta	5.65	-0.47
O1-F7	PHA	Alpha	-3.93	-0.99
F7-F8	PHA	Alpha	-0.74	-0.75
T5-T6	PHA	Beta	9.88	-0.51
C3-F7	AMP	Delta	11.90	-1.04
FP2-F4	AMP	Delta	15.21	0.59
C4-F8	AMP	Delta	-18.61	-2.32
O1-O2	AMP	Theta	-10.47	-0.78
P3-F7	AMP	Alpha	18.31	2.00
FP2-P4	AMP	Alpha	-7.20	1.48

The TBI Severity Index is an estimate of the neurological severity of injury. (see Thatcher et al, J. Neuropsychiatry and Clinical Neuroscience, 13(1): 77-87, 2001.)

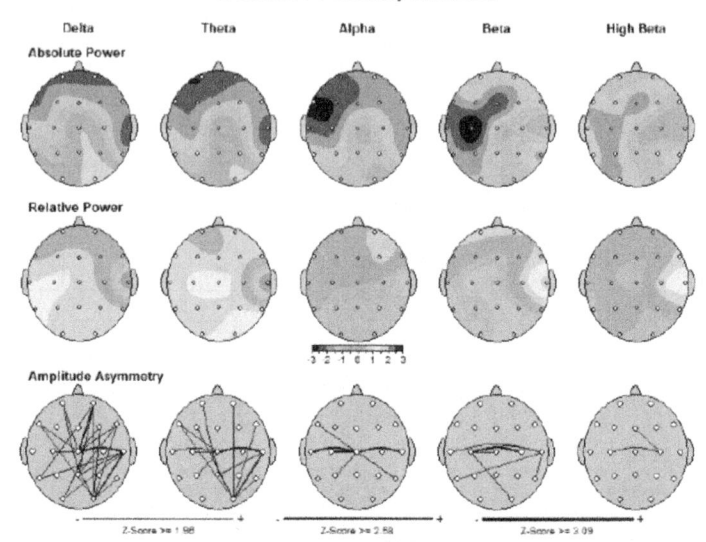

Above image is from August 2019

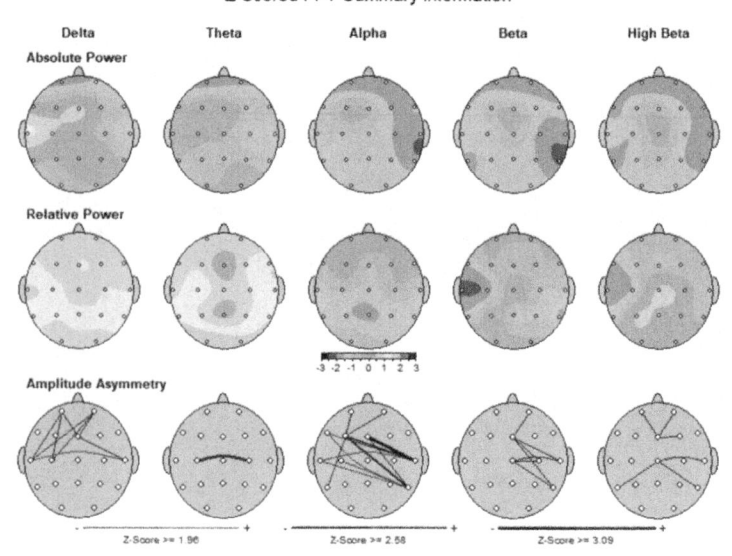

Above image is from December 2019

Cognitive Assessment Report

Assessment Details

ID: matuf23
Gender: Male
Date of Birth: 08/19/1972
Tasks Completed: 12
Completion Date: 08/22/2019 16:42
Comparative Group: Males, 45-54

Performance Summary

Task	Category	Score
Monkey Ladder	Visuospatial Working Memory	118
Spatial Span	Spatial Short-Term Memory	107
Token Search	Working Memory	107
Paired Associates	Episodic Memory	106
Rotations	Mental Rotation	104
Polygons	Visuospatial Processing	106
Odd One Out	Deductive Reasoning	105
Spatial Planning	Planning	96
Grammatical Reasoning	Verbal Reasoning	107
Digit Span	Verbal Short-Term Memory	106
Feature Match	Attention	96
Double Trouble	Response Inhibition	122

CBS Health is not a diagnostic tool. CBS Health provides a scientifically-validated and objective measure of cognitive function and should be used in conjunction with other information and clinical judgement to reach the appropriate conclusions regarding an individual's health. CBS Health does not replace the judgement of a practitioner and Cambridge Brain Sciences does not assume responsibility for the outcome of decisions made based on CBS Health data.

Cognitive Assessment Report

Powered By CAMBRIDGE BRAIN SCIENCES

Assessment Details

ID:	matul23	Tasks Completed:	12
Gender:	Male	Completion Date:	03/07/2020 11:11
Date of Birth:	08/19/1972	Comparative Group:	Males, 45-54

Performance Summary

Below Average — 87 — Average — 113 — Above Average

Task	Domain	Score
Monkey Ladder	Visuospatial Working Memory	118
Spatial Span	Spatial Short-Term Memory	114
Token Search	Working Memory	112
Paired Associates	Episodic Memory	102
Rotations	Mental Rotation	119
Polygons	Visuospatial Processing	105
Odd One Out	Deductive Reasoning	109
Spatial Planning	Planning	128
Grammatical Reasoning	Verbal Reasoning	109
Digit Span	Verbal Short-Term Memory	107
Feature Match	Attention	93
Double Trouble	Response Inhibition	119

CBS Health is not a diagnostic tool. CBS Health provides a scientifically-validated and objective measure of cognitive function and should be used in conjunction with other information and clinical judgement to reach the appropriate conclusions regarding an individual's health. CBS Health does not replace the judgement of a practitioner and Cambridge Brain Sciences does not assume responsibility for the outcome of decisions made based on CBS Health data.

Millennium TBI Network
Rebuilding Hope one day at a time

ALLERGIES: TBI

Tullius, Mark (46)
Lab Date: 10/25/2018

Hormone Testing	Results	Range			04/19/18
Growth Hormone		4.0ng/ml*			1.45 N
Somatomedin C (IGF-1)*	122 LN	200 ng/ml*			155 N
IGF BP-3	4800 N	4000 ng/ml*			4900 N
DHEA-S**	482.2 HN	~301 ug/dl*			216.1 LN
Testosterone Free**	11.49 LN	~14 pg/ml*			8.14 LN
Testosterone Total	881 N	690 ng/ml*			470 N
Dihydrotestosterone (DHT)	46.3 N	55 ng/Dl*			21.2 N
Sex Hormone Binding Gb	73 HN	45 pg/ml*			42 N
Prostatic PSA		<4.0ng/ml			0.51 N
Estrone (E1)	25.7 N	<60 pg/ml*			14.9 N
Estradiol (E2)	43.2 H	<40 pg/ml*			24.2 N
Pregnenolone**		80-100 ng/dl*			26.2 LN
Progesterone*		0.8ng/ml*			0.46 LN
FSH		7 mIU/ml*			2.4 LN
Luteinizing Hormone**	4.6 N	5.1 mIU/ml			3.2 LN
Prolactin**		14 ng/ml*			6.4 LN
Zinc		95 mcg/dL*			87 N
Insulin		<25mIU/L			3.6 N
Vitamin D3***		80-100 ng/dl*			28 L
TSH		<2.5 mcu/ml*			2.98 HN
T4, Free		1.5 ng/ml			1.28 LN
TSH Index		1.3 – 4.1			3.15 N
T3, Free		2.5 pg/ml			3.0 N
rT3		80-250 pg/ml			152 N
T3/rT3 Ratio		>1.06			1.97 N
TPO		<35			-
ACTH		<35pg/ml*			-
Cortisol		<15 ug/dl			8.6 N

* The IDEAL RANGE is at the 50th percentile of optimal. Treatment is geared to 50th – 75th percentile.

REVIEW

If you enjoyed this book, I hope you'll take a moment to write a quick review. As an independent author, word of mouth and reviews are incredibly helpful. Whether you leave one star or five, honest feedback is truly appreciated. And if you're on Goodreads or BookBub please stalk me. I believe the technical term is Follow, but I strive on anxiety and what better way to amp it up than thinking there are hundreds of strangers stalking me. Plus, you'll be alerted to all my new books and deals. Sounds like a win-win to me.

Here is the link to leave a review on Amazon:
https://amzn.to/3sNvgr5

Here is the link to leave a review on Goodreads:
https://www.goodreads.com/book/show/59493919-tbi-or-cte

Thank you!

ABOUT THE AUTHOR

Mark Tullius is the author of *TBI or CTE: What the Hell is Wrong with Me?*, *Unlocking the Cage*, *Ain't No Messiah*, *Twisted Reunion*, *25 Perfect Days*, the *Brightside* series, and the creator of the *Try Not to Die* series. Mark resides in Southern California with his wife and two children.

Website - www.MarkTullius.com
Podcast - https://viciouswhispers.podbean.com
Instagram - @author_mark_tullius
Facebook – http://www.facebook.com/AuthorMarkTullius
Twitter - https://twitter.com/MarkTullius
Youtube – http://www.youtube.com/MarkTullius

Out Now - TNTD: In the Wizard's Tower

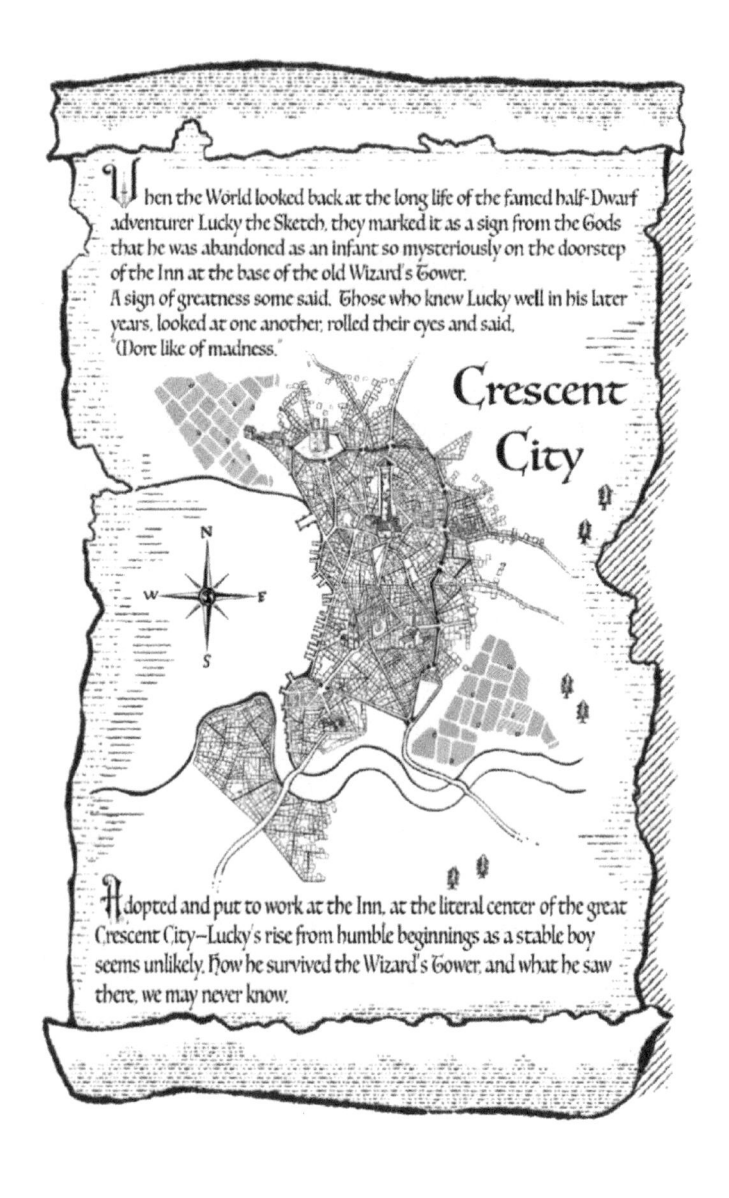

When the World looked back at the long life of the famed half-Dwarf adventurer Lucky the Sketch, they marked it as a sign from the Gods that he was abandoned as an infant so mysteriously on the doorstep of the Inn at the base of the old Wizard's Tower.
A sign of greatness some said. Those who knew Lucky well in his later years, looked at one another, rolled their eyes and said, "More like of madness."

Crescent City

Adopted and put to work at the Inn, at the literal center of the great Crescent City–Lucky's rise from humble beginnings as a stable boy seems unlikely. How he survived the Wizard's Tower, and what he saw there, we may never know.

Coming Soon from Vincere Press

Try Not to Die: Super High

Summer 2022: Mark and Steve Montgomery team up to bring the Try Not to Die series to Florida. Become a young competitive sharpshooter and enjoy a night out in Miami. Just don't get bit by any of the bath salt people.

Try Not to Die: In the Wild West

Fall 2022: Mark and John Palisano reunite to bring the first western to the Try Not to Die series.

Tales of the Blessed and Broken: The Early Years

A collection of 27 short stories set in the Tales of the Blessed and Broken world. Take a look at the childhoods of three protagonists from the 5-book series: Heimdall, Lucas, and Vincent.

Out Now from Vincere Press

FICTION

Try Not to Die: Books 1-3

Get the first three books in the series. TNTD: At Grandma's House, In Brightside, and In the Pandemic.

Try Not to Die: In the Wizard's Tower

Your name is Lucky. Your entire life you have lived at the Inn at the base of the impenetrable Wizard's Tower. But now you're stuck inside the mysterious Tower, mercy to its puzzles, traps, creatures...and magic.

Brightside

Across the nation, telepaths are rounded up and sent to the beautiful mountain town of Brightside. They're told it's just like everywhere else, probably even nicer. As long as they follow the rules and don't ever think about leaving. Joe Nolan is one of the accused, a man who spent his life hearing things people left unsaid. And now he's paying for it on his hundredth day in Brightside, fighting to keep hold of his secret in a town where no thought is safe.

Beyond Brightside

The exciting conclusion to the Brightside saga. Joe and Becky thought life was hard in Brightside, but beyond Brightside is even more brutal.

A Dark and Disturbing Collection

A boxset that includes 82 short stories taken from *Twisted Reunion*, *Untold Mayhem*, and *25 Perfect Days: Plus 5 More*.

Ain't No Messiah

The coming of age psychological thriller about Joshua Campbell: a man of death-defying miracles, whose father proclaimed him the Second Coming of Christ.

Follow Joshua through a childhood of physical and emotional abuse, and into adulthood as he attempts to break away from his family and church in order to find happiness.

Nonfiction

Unlocking the Cage: Exploring the Motivations of MMA Fighters

For his first nonfiction project, Tullius spent 3 years traveling to 23 states and visiting 100 gyms where he interviewed 340 fighters in his search to understand who MMA fighters are and why they fight.

"The result is a surprisingly revealing read recommended not just for enthusiasts of boxing, fighting, and MMA in particular, but especially for outsiders who abhor the idea of such a sport without really understanding its players. This audience will find their eyes opened about many things, including evolving values and maturity processes in life, and will discover Unlocking the Cage also unlocks preconceived notions about a little-understood sport." - D.Donovan, Senior Reviewer, Midwest Book Review

AND DON'T MISS

VICIOUS WHISPERS PODCAST

To hear free audiobooks and listen to Mark's weekly rant, be sure to look for his podcast, *Vicious Whispers with Mark Tullius* which you can find on YouTube, iTunes, Spotify, Stitcher and other places podcasts are played.

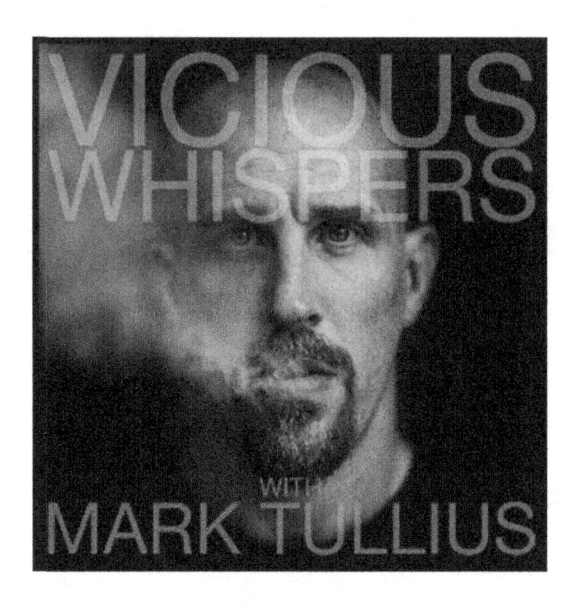

https://viciouswhispers.podbean.com

Your Free Book is Waiting

Three short horror stories and one piece of nonfiction by Mark Tullius, one of the hardest-hitting authors around. The tales are bound to leave you more than a touch unsettled.

Get to know:

- an overweight father ignored by his family and paying the ultimate and unexpected price for his sins

- a gang member breaking into a neighborhood church despite the nagging feeling that something about the situation is desperately wrong

- a cameraman who finds himself in a hopeless situation after his involvement in exposing a sex trafficking ring

- the aging author paying the price for a reckless past, now doing all he can to repair his brain

These shocking stories will leave you wanting more.
Get a free copy of this collection.
Morsels of Mayhem: An Unsettling Appetizer here:
https://www.marktullius.com/free-book-is-waiting

Made in United States
Orlando, FL
06 May 2023